1

# The Rhyme Traveller

Poems and Illustrations

by

Richard Charles Calverley Crabtree

British Library Cataloguing in Publication Data.

A catalogue record for this book is available from the British Library.

ISBN 978-1-3999-7059-4

| | | |
|---|---|---|
| Previous publications | - *Wild Oats* | 1976 |
| Reprinted | - *Wild Oats* | 1977 |
| | - *Mickey Finn* | 1978 |
| | - *Fox Night* | 1983 |

# NOTES BY THE AUTHOR

The Yorkshire Arts Association (YAA) was greatly influential in the 1970s and 1980s by providing both encouragement and the means to print, publish and distribute my first three books, *Wild Oats*, *Mickey Finn* and *Fox Night*.

Those books are now out of print, and the YAA has long since been swallowed up by the Arts Council of Great Britain. But those early years working with both the YAA and the Sheffield Poetry Workshop led me to progress in becoming a regular contributor to *Peak Advertiser*, a highly regarded local publication with a wide circulation of over 25000 copies each fortnight within the Derbyshire Dales. *Peak Advertiser* has published over 300 of my poems and illustrations spanning the past twenty years. My poetry has also been read on BBC Radio, appeared in the national media and has won awards.

I was born in Yorkshire in 1945 and attended school there, but much of my boyhood and early adult life was spent living and working in the High Peak of Derbyshire. I have a shared love of Yorkshire, the Peak District and the North Norfolk coast, where I now live, and all have influenced my poetry.

My lifetime has seen the greatest advancements of any previous generation. As a boy, few families had a car, and fewer still had TV. Computers would fill a room and were not available to the masses. There were no mobile phones, the first heart transplant was twenty-odd years in the future and my dad was born too soon.

At that time, there was one TV on our road. The screen was like a bull's eye, but straight after school, a lucky few were invited round to watch Kit Carson. On Saturdays, we often went to the Picture House to watch the morning matinee, featuring cliff-hanging adventures, cartoons and the Pathé News.

In those days, rail travel was by steam, ships had only just followed suit, and air travel was in its infancy. We had only just seen the demise of the Spitfire and the Lancaster bomber, and I went to school on a tram, passing blitzed-out buildings awaiting demolition.

By the time I was twenty, almost every family owned a TV (black and white), every second family owned a car, steam-driven engines were to be phased out in favour of diesel, and air travel had moved into the era of the package holiday. My hometown of Sheffield was still being rebuilt after the heavy Blitz by the Luftwaffe in December 1940. By the age of thirty, computers were beginning to be available, but were not in everyday use. A mobile phone was referred to as a brick and just had one function. Star Trek was on TV, medicine and surgery had taken massive strides forward and most families by then had two cars. Oh … and a real spaceman had landed on the real moon.

As a boy, I read *Eagle*, which told of the exploits of Dan Dare and the evil Mighty Mekon. I knew then that space travel would come true, just as I know now, that in the future we will discover new worlds and that many of my boyhood fantasies will become reality. But firstly, I know that we must protect our own planet from the by-products of those years of advancement and growing human needs. I remember those days when houses were so cold in the winter you could see your own breath. I recall my mum and dad converting our cottage from gas lighting to electricity, and mum doing the weekly wash on a Monday, by hand and with a mangle. We did not have domestic freezers then, but our pantry was piled high with things in tins, just in case of another war. As children, we still played with toys, and imagined. We are all time-travellers, from the day we are born to the day we die, and we all have a built-in time machine comprising two moving parts – memory and imagination. Through memory, we can recall the past; with imagination, we can time-travel beyond any boundary or constraint. The following book represents one person's time-travel fuelled only by memory, imagination and a social history of events influencing that journey. Imagination has no constraints of time or place; it enables travel fuelled only by the will to seek adventure.

# INFINITELY MORE SPACE

Space, I believe, is infinite.
If it were not,
It would have an edge.
And beyond that … what?
Infinitely more space,
Or one hell of a drop?
And even if surmised
It was round like a ball,
Outside the circumference
There'd still be free-fall.

Into what?

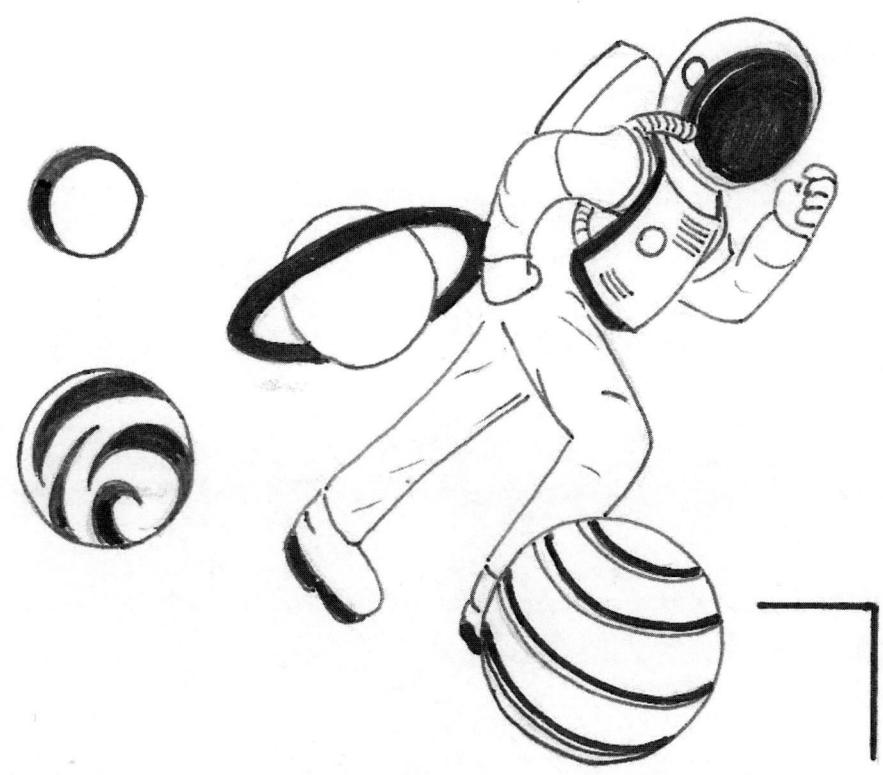

# RAINBOW

When Odin's earth was dark and cold
And blanketed in cumulus,
Spinning in a galaxy where stars of gems were dim,
A sun began to grow and warm,
And all the silent darkness there
Gathered into storm.

And there amid the swirling squall
Knelt Thor in a cloud of gold,
As he rolled along its coloured beam
A wondrous treasure trove.
And as it turned in thunderous roar,
It seemed to cast a light
Of ruby and of emerald
Extracted from the night.

Then, through a diamond, pierced the day
In lightning to the ground,
And indigo and violet hue
Rippled with the sound.

The clearing sky turned sapphire blue
Behind the cloud of gold,
Which left a multi-coloured bridge –
And Thor slid down his treasure trove.

# FOSSILISED

When very first primeval life
Heaved itself on lava shore
And gasped in air,
Invertebrate
Began to turn to dinosaur.

A lung was formed –
Some grew feet, others kept a tail.
Animal amphibians
Evolved
On fishy scale.

Some with fins developed wings
And screeched across volcanic sky,
Terrifying carnivores
With
Pterodactyl cry.

Beneath the sea the legless breeds
Swelled on Ammonoids,
Fought in shoals of
Pliosaur
And Plesiosaurus noise.

While on Cretaceous land above
Now forested in fruit and flower,
Dinosaurian-domination
Reached
Extinction hour.

# THE START

'In the beginning'
A mythical brain,
Like chrysalis,
Outgrew its cave
And caught itself a God.
"I know" – it dreamed,
As it weaved its thought
And dried in the brand-new sun.
"I know" – it dreamed,
And with imaginary rib, the brain
A gleaming body grew.
"Now I can yawn, and stretch
And scratch,
Now I can see with glistening eyes.
Now I can write of wondrous things" –
"Now," he dreamed, "I can tell of this" –
And promptly drafted Genesis.

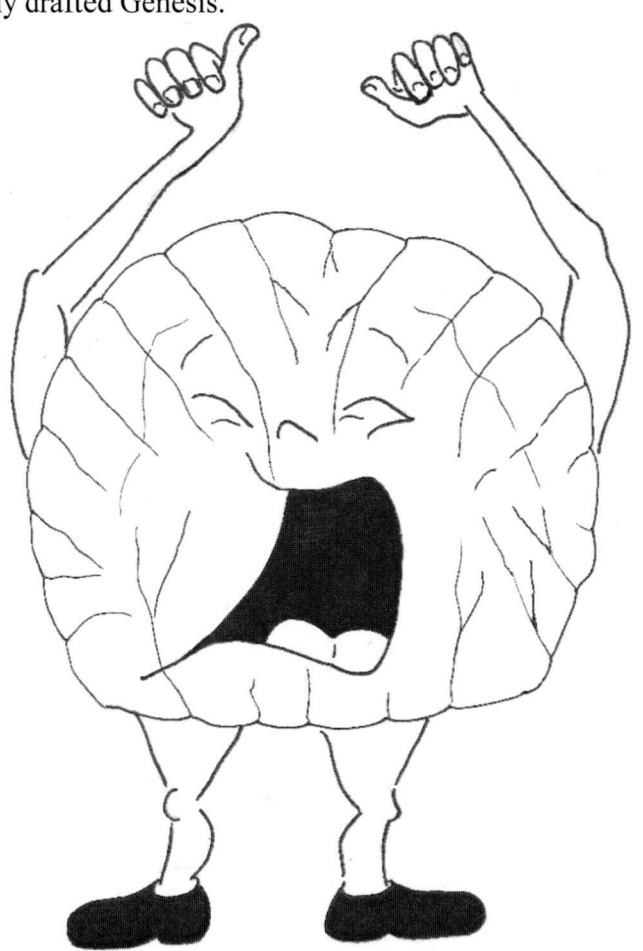

I wrote the following after eating a large Christmas dinner, opening Christmas crackers containing silly jokes, having far too many glasses of wine, and falling asleep during *Jurassic Park*.

I am, of course, aware of the seriousness of dietary disorders and apologise in advance, hoping readers will see the humour of my poem and not take offence.

It all started off when I made a silly Christmas-cracker kind of joke and sketched a cartoon on the back of my napkin to accompany it. Then I went on to write the poem –

Continued

# SKINNY DINOSAUR

She was the cutest dinosaur,
Trim and in her teens.
Until that dreadful day arrived,
She couldn't zip her jeans.
Her teeth they sparkled in the sun,
Eye lashes long and black,
She feared her youth was slipping by –
There was no turning back.
You know how fads they come and go,
She turned veggie overnight,
A leap for a hungry carnivore
To small herbivorous bites.
The pounds fell off, so dull her scales,
She really couldn't stop,
Then thankfully good sense prevailed,
She went to see the Doc'.
He quickly dino-nosed her,
Prescribed for her rare meat,
But the hussy ate his outstretched hand
And then devoured his feet;
Tore off his head and gulped it down,
Then gobbled up the rest,
Saved the bulk until the last
Enjoying it the best!
She quickly piled back on the weight
And soon regained her size,
As others in the surgery
All met with their demise.
There is a moral to this tale,
That if you burst your jeans,
Don't be like our dinosaur
And diet to extremes.

## INSTINCT ONE

INSTINCT
THE LINK
CREATION
SPRINKLED
ON
LIVING
THINGS
FOR
RE-GENERATION
OR
THEY'D
BE EXTINCT
I THINK

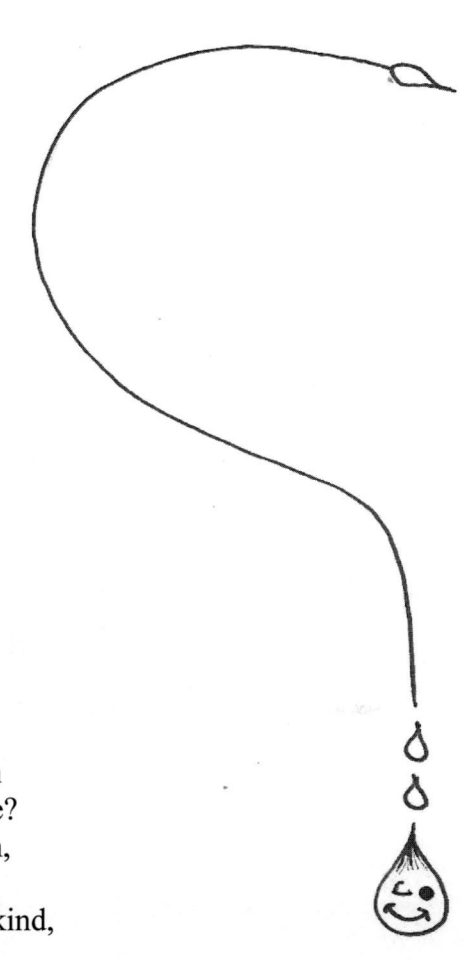

## INSTINCT TWO

In the beginning.
Instinct – the link,
Invisibly installed within
Every species on this earth
And maybe in the universe?
For survival or procreation,
Automatic propagation –
A stardust sprinkling of a kind,
A guaranteed family line;
It is a strange anomaly,
No anatomical ecology,
Just a built-in thing. Instinct.

# VOYEUR CONSTRICTOR

Boastful Adam
Said to Eve –
"We should thank God
For the large fig leaf."
As quick as a snake bite
Eve replied –
"He also made
The smaller size!"
Though why in Eden
One should care,
For who's to see
If they go bare?
Ah, maybe the serpent
Could by chance
Take a slithery
Sideways glance!

So perhaps it's rather
More than luck
The leaves were there
To cover up.

.

# EVE

# THE ARROGANT MONKEY

The Arrogant Monkey
Called himself Man,
Created in the image of … YOU?
He preened his fine coat
And thought to himself,
"I'm not like those apes in the zoo."
He made his own jungle
From trees of desire,
His need became more than a scratch.
YOU provided earth, wind and fire,
And the monkey never looked back.
He then discovered his arrogant Jane
(A derivative of his own kind)
To make other Arrogant Monkeys –
Their particular arrogance combined.
YOU gifted them rain
To make the crops grow,
Which flourished
To give them their food.
The apes reflected how well THEY`D done,
Their arrogance grew and grew.
Their trees of desire
Were made into boats,
Rivets were cast in the fire.
Their hunger and thirst
Were fulfilled by YOU
As desire soared higher and higher.
They grew in their arrogance,
They grew in their needs,
And spread to each end of the Earth.
Raiding, squabbling, thieving –
Planet of the Apes given birth!
Those other more docile monkeys
Still shuffle around in their zoo,
Content with some fruit
And occasional scratch.
But the Arrogant Monkeys,
Aided by YOU,
Forge onward
And never look back.

# THE GARDEN

In the garden
A round white soul
Rolled down a rut-worn path,
Its casing was aged and vulnerable
Like the shell of a natural hive,
And it moved from side to side on its own momentum.
There were many, many other souls,
Some red, yellow or black,
All moving, some in jerks,
Others smoothly and some lay burst,
Where a naked old man
Sat clenching a sharp stick.

The garden was filled with tropical fruit,
Huge orchids and vines.
At night, the old man
Climbed to an apiary,
Where he lodged with giant bees,
Who spun sweet shells in filigree,
Whilst he, carefully
Placed those chosen souls
Back inside.

## POOR NOAH

The day of prophesy arrived,
A giant ark stood ready,
Noah upon the gopher deck
Proud captain fine and steady.
Years of building, plans and toil
Storm clouds swirled around,
Flashing lightning from the skies
Pierced the hardened ground.
He'd herded every beast inside,
In couples of like-kind,
To an 18-30s party boat
Pent-up urges on their minds.
There was every serpent of the earth
And bird that flew the sky,
All insects, plants and forms of life
Gathered there before his eyes.

    Then suddenly –
    Mischievous thought
    Did lead my mind awry –
    Suppose the rains had failed to come,
    Those dark clouds floating by;
    And a heavenly voice
    From the place on high hailed …

    "Come on Noah (♫ Dum de dum, de dum de dum de dum ♫)
    Always look on the bright side of life!"

Footnote:
1. Has anyone got a shovel?
2. A bucket of cold water?
3. Transportation to the med'?
4. Oh Arksouls!

## SLING KING

David when standing before Goliath
Faced a fine dividing-line
Between defiant demonstration
Of giant annihilation
And just looking – – – – – – STUPID.
The moral being,
If you're small
And the target's tall, stop to consider this:
What could happen if you miss?
But it's worth a go –
No effort, no gain.
So, take careful aim,
It'll all be worth it when you've won.
But if you fail, be sure to run.
Vacate the scene!
David would have,
I mean …
Just look at the size of that Goliath!

# ODDS OR EVENS

Sometimes in life, depending on how the dice fall, we can find ourselves in the most dreadful situations, where we tolerate all manner of difficulties – until hopefully, from somewhere within, we gather the strength, figuratively speaking, to overturn the table.

Half goat, hob-foot and horned,
He crouched, servant at his side,
Red eyes cast to the dice.
Odds or evens?
"Odds are mine!" He screamed,
And threw a three –
"Evens for you,
Odds for me!" He flamed
From a smouldering demon throat,
And rolled the dice again.
"A two, three and two makes five!"
At the other side
Of a half-molten table,
In white and gold bearded heaven,
Sat a beaten man,
Chips down,
Head hung
In curls and frown.
He'd thought carefully,
More than twice,
But knew he'd lost
Before he tossed
The dice.
First a six
And then a five.
"Six and five's eleven,"
Chanted the black blood-eyed gibbon,
Shoulder high at his master's side –
And snatched back the dice from heaven.
"Another for us," scoffed Beelzebub.
"Why don't you cheat?"
Blasted a flame-voice from the heat.
And the man grew
Strong and tall
And overturned the table.

20

# CROSSWORD

IN MY FOLLOWING CONCRETE (OR VISUAL) POEM, *CROSSWORD*, TWO SHOCKING FORMS OF DEATH ARE DEPICTED IN THE PERFECT FORM OF A CROSS – THE CROSS BEING A SYMBOL WITHIN THE CHRISTIAN CHURCH OF AN ALL-FORGIVING GOD.

STONE GUN

Petrified
Now without fear
A lone soldier
Stands at ease
In the frozen park.
His grey eyes stare
Perplexed
At a stone gun
As the cold
Breath
Of Somme
Dies
Within
Him.

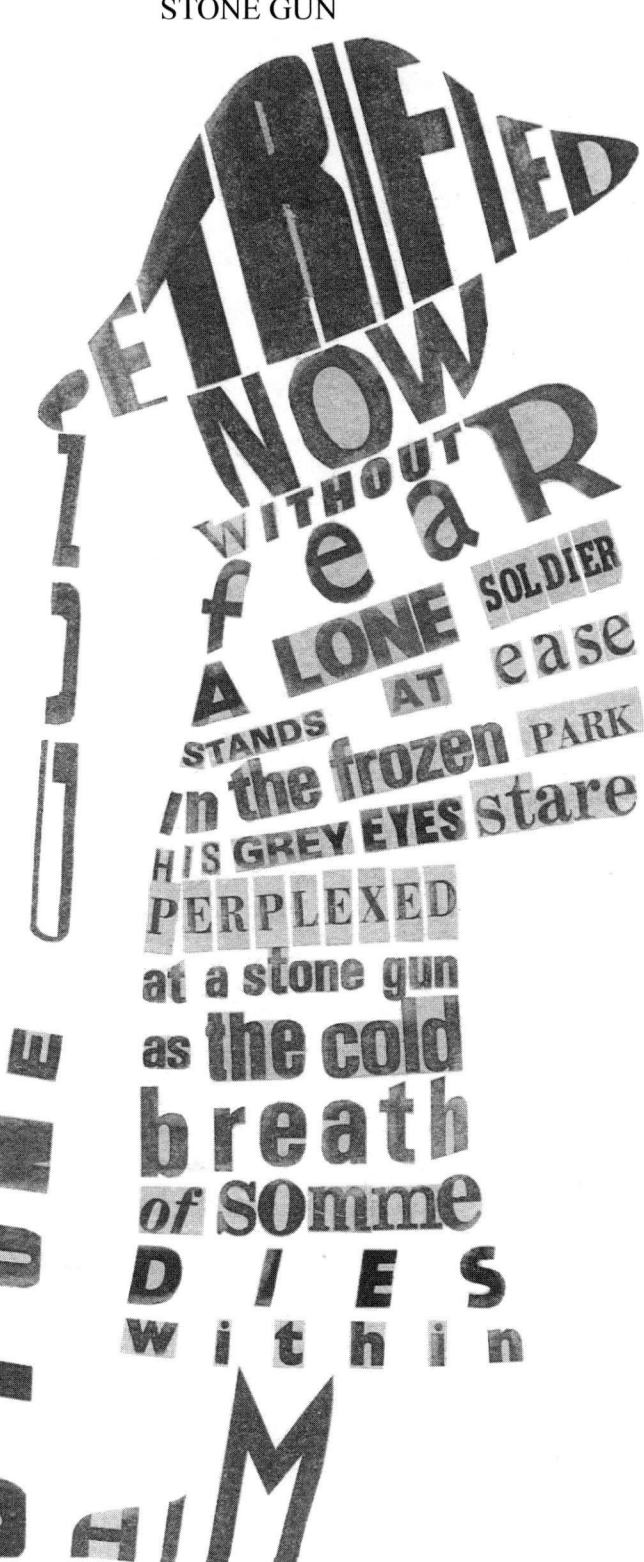

## "YOU CHAPS COULD TURN THE TIDE"
### Opening Night – Act One.

How did I arrive in such a grim place
To clamber upon that wretched stage,
Where a dark impatient audience waits;
Until those black curtains whistle back,
And we blunder toward that harnessed roar
Of deafening applause,
To a novice act of war?
Believing we could not die
Each quelling a cold stage fright,
We ran towards those glaring lights
Fully intending to fight –
We put on a good show,
My comrades and I,
On that final opening night.
We could not question why
Or the validity of lies,
But just played our parts
In the tragedy.
"You chaps could turn the tide" –
There were liars and heroes
On either side.
Those liars were somewhere
Out of sight,
As the futile script
Was re-written for all,
By oh so many heroes' lives.

# FLANDERS

Amongst the gaping-mouthed craters
And those disfigured places
Where level meadow grass had been,
That once unsullied earth
Was tainted,
Awash with mingled blood –
Red,
Where it once was green.
And that scorched land,
Now purged
Of the folly of man,
Will forever be
A sorrier scene.
And where the air was gas and death,
Open wounds
As yet unhealed,
A dreadful sadness swept that place.
No winners
Left that field.

Rupert Brook

Francis Ledwidge

Siegfried Sassoon

Edmund Blunden

Philip Thomas

## WAR POETS' EYES

War poets' eyes,
All fixed on distant skies,
Far beyond their vision.

Safe, where those who made decisions
Sheltered, out of range;
A place of ever-shifting blame,
Where words of war were soon denied
And reasons lay in a trench of lies.

But on that land, where wisdom failed –
    No man should be where hate prevails
And those who just obeyed command
Could never truly understand…

Why.

And now, it's there for all – frame-freezed
In photographs. Come, look and see …

The whys –

    It's clear within the war poets' eyes.

In summer 2014, I watched a remembrance service on TV, which marked the centenary of the start of World War I. Various celebrities read poetry in the presence of a congregation that included royalty, politicians and leaders of the armed forces. The remembrance service, which was very moving, left me in no doubt of the potential power of the pen; or as Edward George Bulwer Lytton wrote, "The pen is mightier than the sword." If only!

## FEARS AND HEROES

We remember and honour those heroes of war,
Who fight – without question of orders – no more.
Whose unfulfilled but obedient lives
Paid unearned debts of sacrifice.
And within that peace they now abide,
Their fears remain silenced where they died.

For fears and heroes are two of a kind,
With a very harsh dividing line.

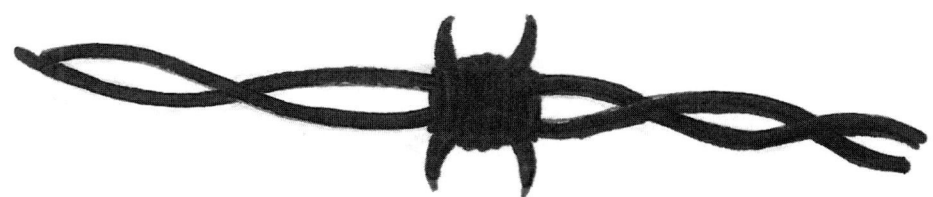

# RETURN TO DUNKIRK

"How many lives shall be lost?"

Thought the old man, as he tossed
A pebble high in the air
And caught it on the back of his stoney hand.

His thin fingers stretched out
Like the long years behind him,
And the places that had forever changed.

He remembered the dull sound of guns,
Faces in a long marching row,
As he watched children who would never know
How it had been.

Deep in thought, he cast two pebbles
Again, high in the air.
And once more caught both with great care –
Not to lose a life.

Alexander McKay died just there,
Where the children sculpted the blood-soaked sand,
Once grasped in an outstretched hand
In a last reach for home.

Tossing three pebbles, then four,
He skilfully caught all.
Still lost in his thoughts of war,
The old man gathered up five pebbles
And squeezed them all
Tightly in his hand, lest they should fall.


"Five-stones is a game for children or old fools," he thought.

# CHURCHILL'S TEETH

Never in the field of human teeth
Had so much been offered
By so many
For so few.

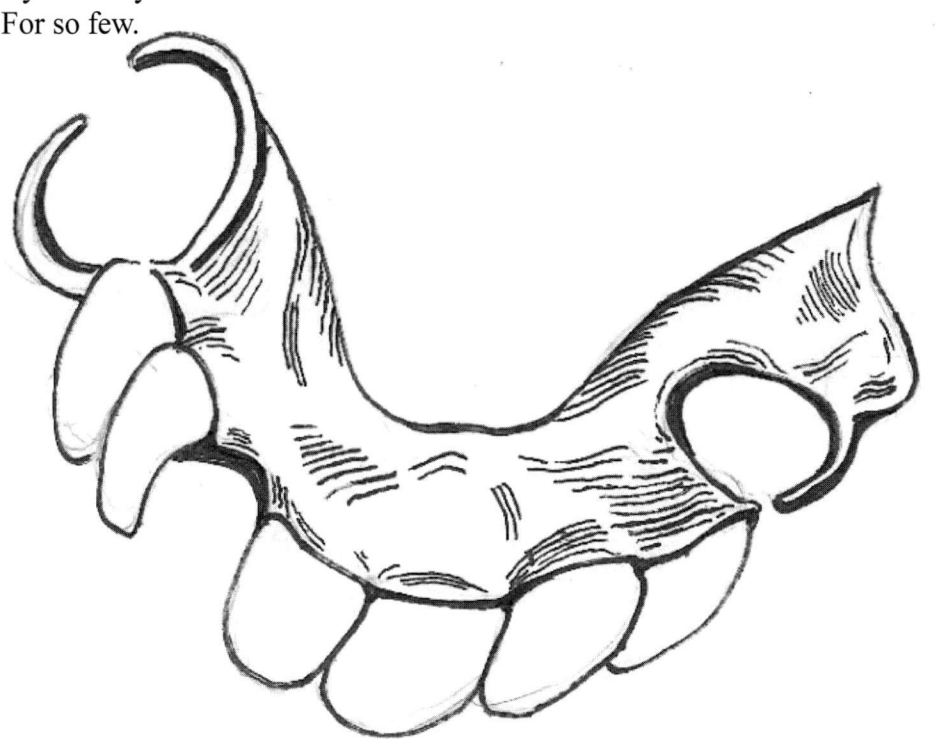

WITH APOLOGIES TO THOSE HEROES OF THE BATTLE OF BRITAIN
…

In 2010, Winston Churchill's teeth sold at auction for the jaw-dropping sum of £15,200. Apparently, they were specially designed to preserve his natural lisp, and he always carried two pairs with him.

My poem was inspired by one of his greatest speeches:

"Never in the field of human conflict was so much owed by so many to so few."

I think there would be a slim chance of war, if those opposing decision makers were made to fight it out in person at the O.K. Corral – Move over Wyatt!

## OK CORRAL

OK, so it's almost time
To defend those decisions –
Here's some Colt 45s
And boxed ammunition.
To each of the sides
Guns and rifles are given
As they falteringly stride
To opposing positions.
Risk their own lives,
Those bold politicians?
Now armed and in line,
There's a scene of derision.
What seemed OK – fine –
Disconcertingly isn't.
This isn't OK … is it?

# ‘TIL

’Til the reasons for war are not justified
’Til the causes of war are not denied
’Til the mongers of war discontinue to lie
’Til the soldiers of war discontinue to die
’Til the mothers of war discontinue to cry

’Til …

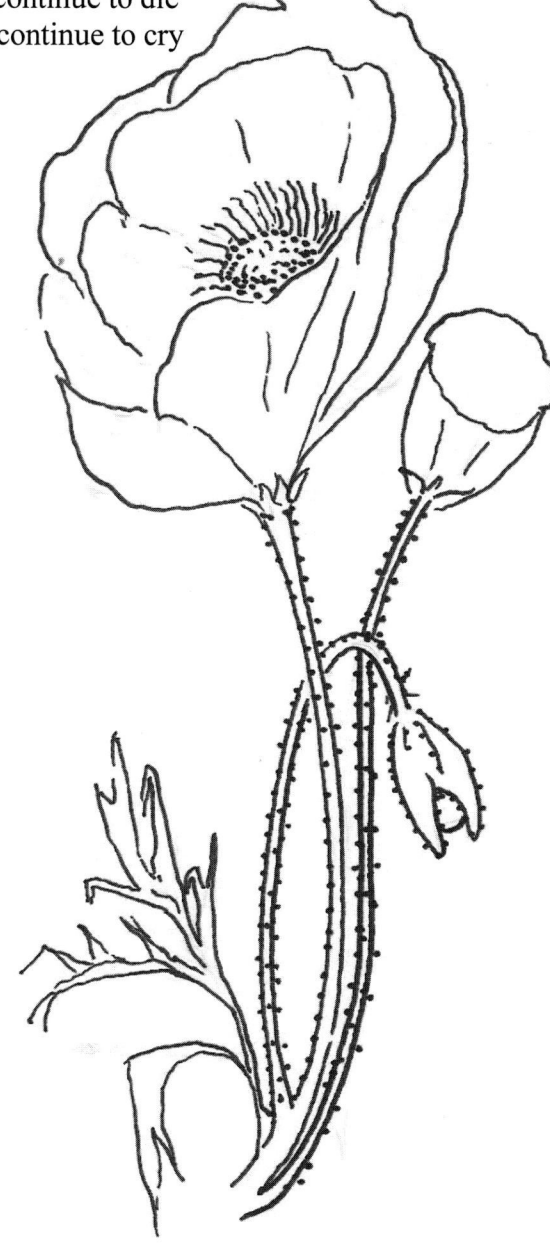

# DOVE OF PEACE

Verbal entrenchments,
Minefields between each,
Differences
Too wide to breach.
Assaults from the landing
Lay dead on the beach,
Hands stretched out
To hope beyond reach,
Until the blindness of war
Sees the white dove of peace.

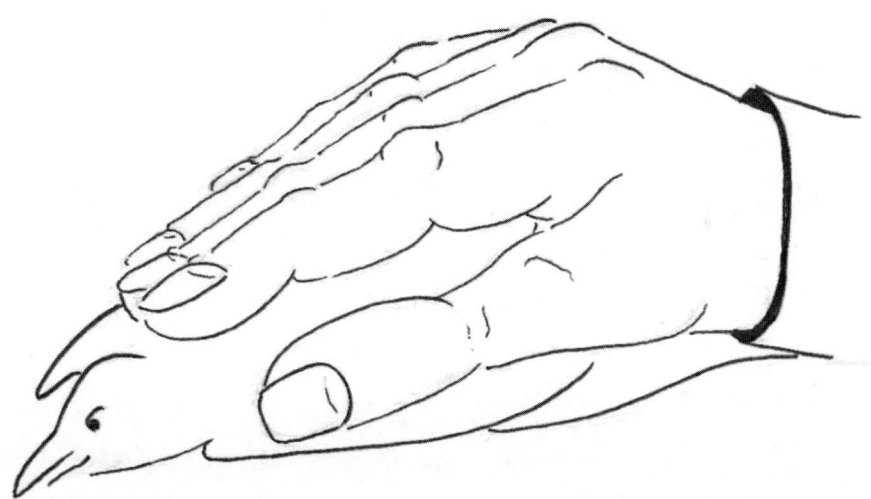

## SCULPTORS OF TODAY
## (BEACH WALK TO WEYBOURNE)

Playful waves trip one another,
Childlike gurgling, girl-like giggling,
Scrambling back over shining flint.
Gleaning bright pebbles, shells and amber,
Trading bottles, driftwood, and orange string.
Relentless teasing, never yielding,
Sieging yesterday's castle display,
Engineered by loving dads –
Wiped clean, for sculptors of today.

Playful gulls chase one another,
Skipping, fidgeting, busily sorting,
Humble jumble of the tide.
Lugworm, crab, and arctic tern,
Keen to spoil and disarray
Sand rolled level by heavy sea –
Wiped clean, for sculptors of today.

Vengeful men fought one another
From this concrete look-out tower,
Tippled from the crumbling cliff,
Canute-like at the water's edge,
Dethroned by nature's power.
Bits of alloy, mines and wire
Remind us of those days' affray.
The guns are silent now –
Wiped clean, for sculptors of today.

# POTTY POEM

When I was just a little lad
Oft' sat upon a potty,
Gathering in pinkish tones
Rings around my botty.

With cheeks so red and pursed forehead
Puckering in frown,
I crouched like Buddha in a trance
Enthroned in dressing gown.

# A CHILD'S BEDTIME IN SUBURBIA

From within those darkened confines
Of his old bedroom and time,
George could still harken
That clear birdsong of freedom,
See Summer's drawn-out daylight
Behind closed curtains,
Where children's voices sang aloud
To play out late.
He recalled the sounds of cricket –
Shouts of "ow's 'at"
As the wickets fell,
And those older kids' yells of youth,
Which quickly ran to teens
Only to fall like the bails
To family life, mortgage,
Husband or wife,
And maybe, suburbia?

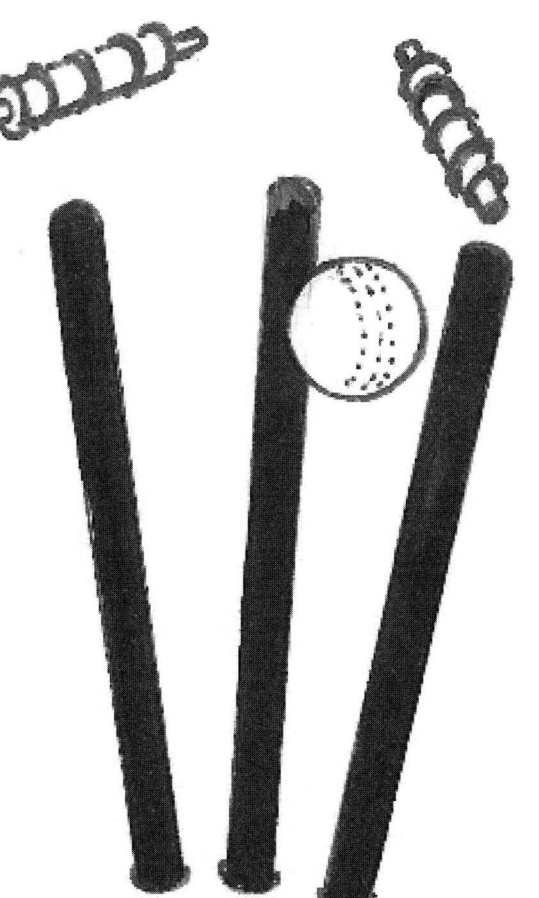

As a young boy – many years before Mrs Thatcher brought an end to coal mining as it was then – I was taken almost every Easter to stay with my great aunt Ethel, who was by then a retired district nurse living in the small village of Stanley, near Wakefield – an area much dependent on the mining industry. My aunt was always early to rise, in time to set the Yorkshire Range and prepare breakfast to the sound of her old valve radio (did it always play *Easter Parade* by Bing?)

Stanley Church overlooked the village in a bleak dominating way, and on Easter Sunday the bells pealed loudly, beckoning the local congregation. Aunt Ethel had painted our hard-boiled eggs in pastel colours, but I couldn't wait to move on to the chocolate ones, and I looked forward to an exciting visit to the cinema just over the road.

My aunt's cottage was next to a tiny smallholding, sharing the yard with just a few chickens and a pig. I remember two young girls waiting by a five-bar gate for their dad to come home from the nearby pit, and his welcome return, black with coal dust and wearing pit helmet and knee pads strapped around his baggy trousers.

Many years after the demise of my great aunt and my parents, I did return to Stanley – then a short detour off the M1. Aunt Ethel's cottage was still there, just to the side of Aberford Road. But the smallholding had been developed into affordable housing, and the cinema to a carpet warehouse.

Stanley Church still dominated the village, just as I remembered.

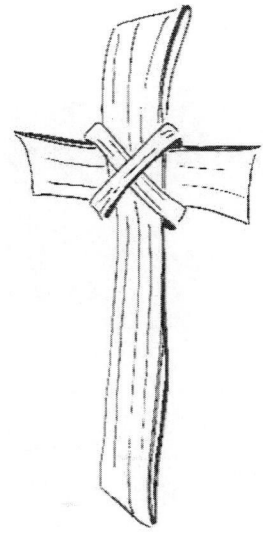

Continued

## STANLEY CHURCH AT EASTERTIDE (NEAR WAKEFIELD)

Dad were hauled up blackened shaft,
Then scrubbed and slicked for Easter Mass,
We were trussed in brand new suits,
And Ma wore bonnet trimmed wi' fruit.
I'll non forget 'ow proud we strolled
To Stanley Church up Aberford Road.
Old Jack, on organ, fair played a treat,
And Psalm twenty-one were 'is masterpiece.
Mr Savage an' Nurse were there,
Colliery boss-cum-Wakefield Mayor,
And all manner o' folk I knew.
Parson had retired to Mickley,
And new 'un had just arrived.
They reckoned he'd come from Otley
And this were 'is testing time.
I thought he were good 'cos he picked hymns I knew,
And his sermons went right well.
He passed his life to
Stanley Church that day –
Though none could tell.
Jack played us out to a better world,
"Our blest Redeemer, ere he breathed".
We all were given a gold edged card
And a fashioned cross of dried palm leaves.
It were '66 when t'pit played out;
Dad had died in '62.
Savage were taken soon after Nurse,
Old Jack 'ad passed on too.
It were '85, an' year Ma died,
I were back in Stanley at Eastertide.

I wrote the following poem sometime in the 1980s, when the Sheffield trams were being phased out in favour of the buses, and the city's new Supertram was still under wraps. At that time, I was living on the outskirts of Sheffield, in the neighbouring Peak District, not too far from the small village of Crich (Pronounced Criche) near Matlock. Crich would probably have remained one of the many hidden jewels of the Derbyshire Peaks, had it not become the end of the line and retirement home for trams.

Crich is now the home of The National Tramway Museum, housing over sixty fine examples of working tramcars built between 1873 and 1982. The museum is set within a recreated period village with its own pub, café, old-style sweetshop and authentic tram depots. The attraction draws visitors from all over the globe.

My poem is set in the 1950s, when tramcars were the main method of commuting in Sheffield. Hundreds of trams, miles of tramlines and overhead cables dominated the city, linking suburbs and inner-city locations like an arterial network. Tram shelters covered queues of anxious passengers waiting to cram inside, to sit, if lucky, or to stand, gripping a precarious overhead stirrup-like handle that slid along a bar as they were ushered further into the tram to make room for more and more passengers. As a boy, I was not tall enough to reach the stirrup, and standing for adults was a requirement that accompanied the school uniform, so I had to cling onto the edge of a seat and develop a knack for balance. My school was located five miles across the city centre and involved a change of tram. The epic journeys to and fro often took an hour each way, but I loved the experience. Some of the trams were constructed pre-war, but as my junior schooldays passed by, new improved models came along, until both the trams and I moved on. The year was 1956. Elvis had released Heartbreak Hotel and emerged on the Ed Sullivan show as one of the World's first rock stars, and I had just passed my eleven-plus to Senior School. But after another five years of commuting across the city, buses had taken over the route.

Sheffield was still fighting its way back from the heavy Luftwaffe bombing it endured in 1940, and over those following sixteen years of the heyday of trams, people had developed a new desire for the ownership of their very own motor car.

Poems, in general, should need no introduction, but on this occasion, I wanted to illustrate yet another example of progress, in what seems such a short passage of time, for this somewhat ancient Rhyme Traveller.

Continued

# TRAVELLING BY TRAMCAR IN SHEFFIELD

I think it's a shame about us trams, don't you?
But I reckon they salvaged more than a few,
For sentiment, tha knows, for them to display.
But there's many of us, can savour the day…

When with a coupl'a penny-uns, and a lass for a lark
Tha could go from the city to Meersbrook Park
Or to Heeley and Woodseats, or Meadowhead.
But if tha were rich, and tha'd got two-and-six,
Tha could jump off at 'The Palace' instead.

I remember the sways, the judders and creaks,
The "Tickets please" and "Feet off the seats!"
"Move down the car! There's two up top.
Hold on tight. Town Hall next stop."

In winter's ice, and covering snow,
They'd steadfast hold their lines,
Hither and thither, and to-and-fro –
Taking you there, and back, on time!

I wonder how many lay fast asleep,
Tucked up in their shed that night,
With but a blinkered, single eye,
And blind to their oncoming plight?
As unaware as the dinosaurs
Of their doom, by meteorite.

But the fate of us trams, were far slower sealed
by the plotting of corporate men,
And the council's ambitions were finally revealed
To make sure
That they ne'er ran again.

# SUNDAY BAND

At first
Sunday morning meant
"The Eagle",
The smell of car polish –
And the church band,
Pathetically Christian.
The Boy's Brigade, with
Pompous military leaders –
Polished, sashed,
(One hurled a mace)
And the line
Diminished into
Out-of-step children,
Half-uniformed.
Some days my scalp
Shrank
To the sound of
The Sunday Band.

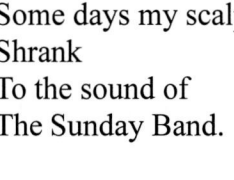

# PRINCESS PEARL AND KING GEORGE

My sister Patricia had two dolls, one was black and the other white,
and they cowered out of sight in the wardrobe.
Once, clutched inside an air-raid shelter,
They'd survived the blitz –
Frightening incendiaries of Fritz,
Only to remain in blackout.
My sister being my elder
Had long-discarded once loved toys,
Her own bombsights then targeted
Earnestly on boys,
And I was only seven.
And those loyal comrades who served in arms,
Unscathed by the passing years,
Broken hearts or teenage tears,
Lay quietly forgotten.

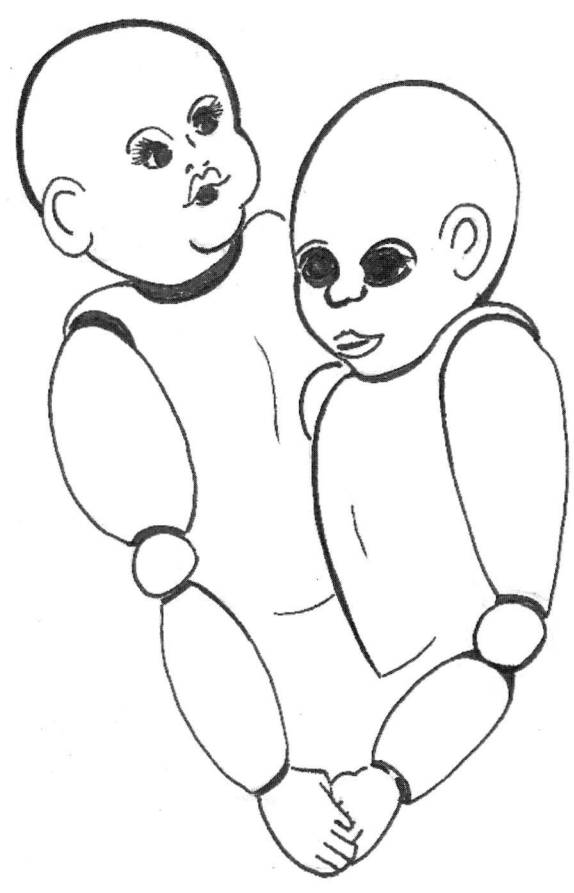

# TRAINSPOTTERS

They often stood on Woodseats' Footbridge,
Waiting for the Six-Fifteen,
'Til the down line MASTER CUTLER
Underneath them screamed
And left those black-faced spotter boys'
Trousers filled with steam!

# THE PALMERS' HUT

The Palmers' hut
Had a locking device –
A long rod of high-tensile steel
Injected through the side.

Seymour worked in steel design.

Inside hung French Onions,
Crab-hard garden gloves,
And symmetrical tools.

The smell was unique
To the Palmers' hut –
It was of cedarwood preservative,
Grass box,
And French onions.

To one side of the hut
Was a bike –
A 'Hercules'.
Everything was surgically
Symmetrical.
There was a chest of drawers,
Each trapping
A long summer day.

They never had a garage,
The Palmers.
They never had a car!

# TO RUPERT

If I'd not read Rupert as a boy, I may have written prose divine,
But Bill the Badger, Algy and Co, set me on the road to Rhyme!
Being a lazy sort of lad, and easily bored with script,
I only read the couplets underneath the pics.
So now I have to think ahead only just one line –
But like the Rupert books I read, the couplets have to rhyme!

Featured on BBC Radio Sheffield 19.2.2002

## SINCE GRANDAD CAME TO THE ORCHARD

That may well have been the start of it.
Those rabbit-lit lanes
Scampering in the headlights of the Standard Big Ten,
Remembering even then –
And wondering if reliable driver Dad
Would last forever.
Watching, staring down the funnelled lights,
Picking every pebble, every detail,
And wishing time would stop.
In those days, when every dog was fierce
And table legs were shelter,
And a kiss a fear,
I remembered the chick-yellow light
Cast from the hay-warm barn
On white, new winter,
Lying rectangular across the yard.
And in spring, when March warmed the land
With frail new Easter-wool,
And the lark sang its welcome –
And the summer grass grew,
And was mown in haze,
And the long days drew short,
And long,
And short again,
And people changed,
From linen summer hats
To flat caps
And some to graves.

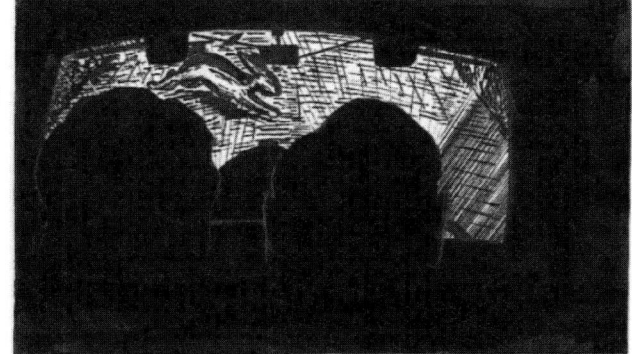

## GRITSTONE FARMER

He taught patience in stone – long grey walls
Dry as time, shaped by men;
Carefully he rebuilt a gap.
He knelt studying like any tutor,
Form – perfection.
Hard hands, bone and stone-weathered
As the eyes of the many builders.
Kind man, the gap is filled,
And the long grey wall still remains.

The day was soft as doe-fur.
A dog sniffed – dry nosed rubble,
Not heeding the moment -
The sound of pipe smoke
And the sight of a laugh …
Vicious time-pup begone!

# JUST A YOLK!

At the height of the storm
When it thundered and lightened
And flashed and it crashed
And the hens all were frightened,
There lay in the coop
An enormous egg
As round as an ostrich's
But twice as big,
And all around the shell
Was a kind of a glow –
The hens stood back
In astonished row.
And just as the storm
Began to subside
The shell grew a crack
And then shattered wide,
And out stepped a hen
Dressed in blue tights and vest,
Embroidered on the front
Was an 'S' on its chest.
SUPERHEN.

FOX
NIGHT

SHORT POEMS
by
RICHARD CRABTREE

*Fox Night*, the title poem of my third book, looks at the subject of instinct, the one thing our creator had to build into every living creature.

The poem combines two of the most sensitive and inexplicable aspects of instinct: motherhood and fear.

As a boy, at Lee Farm in Edale, it was often my job to feed the hens and collect the eggs. In the early evening, I returned to the barn to make sure the poultry were all safely inside, before closing the barn door securely for the night.

The inspiration for this poem came from those days, but after writing it, a boiled egg never seemed quite the same!

Continued

# FOX NIGHT

The shell is a completely
Sealed enclosure – inside
Being totally unexposed to the hen-world
Of bright-eyed scratching
And clucking a whole day long
Until the soft feathered night,
When only a fox-tread
Can be heard from the upturned
Orange box.
Inside the brooding barn
Mothers sit patiently and instinctively
On eggs –
As though they know that
A bright yellow chick will pop out
And call them Mum.
Night holds the barn
Vixen tight
Until dawn shapes
The door.
And a now bold cock,
Head high,
Sounds the all-clear.
From inside shells
Miracles appear,
Suddenly finding the need
To breathe.
Bright-beaked dandelion clocks
Light as air
Trip on stick-legs,
And proud parents
Blink their eyes
And stare.
At last day comes
With a groan
As the huge doors
Crack morning wide open,
And another fox night is done.

# AT NIGHT

When every night was filled with moon
And every moon with owl –
And every fox in silver light
Filled the night with howl,
The child he slept in innocence
And dreamt of a summer day –
When all the world was a rainbow fish
And a new-mown breeze of hay.

# BEFORE I LEFT HOME

When I gulped my first soft breath of air
In a huge yellow beak
And yawned widely
In demand for a meal,
I could feel the sudden presence
Of a quick-winged,
Sleek and beautiful
Mother-bird
Hovering a worm overhead.
I shouted 'food, food'
Till the push of instinct
Was fulfilled
And my round pink tum
Swelled.
The spring days passed
In rain that splashed
Our fat eyes,
Ever fixed upon the sky,
Waiting beak-wide
For more and more food.
My pink tum was now
Spiked with sparse plume,
And room in the nest was short.
I watched the others change
From repulsive worm-fat
Sister and brother
To Sturnus fluffy reflection
Of Mother –
I imagined I'd been the same.
One day the sun
Warmed the nest
Until forced out like
The big green leaves,
We all sat in a line –
Filling our hearts with light
And the will to fly.

# THE TRACTOR

Dawn had breathed into being,
And the old barn door
Cracked against a membrane of silence.
Even the bleary bantam cock
Had not yet stirred, to hurl
Its heralding throat to the day.
That unforgettable warm smell
Of sacks and kerosene
Cosseted the dull-red tractor.
Huge tyres caked in
Shrunken cubes of soil
Pressed from the fragile ground.
The barn was filled
With wondrous, incongruous
Unwanted things,
Some cobwebbed.
Delicate white strands
Reached across the exhaust-stained window.
Half-filled jam jars
Of dried marking fluid
Impaled with the remnant
Of a bark-stripped stick.
Rusted iron objects –
Agricultural, mechanical –
Long gone the machine;
All but the dull-red tractor.
I longed to clean it,
Shining bright-red,
But no –
It was,
In a way, artistic –
More so than a team,
And the dull weather-worn red paint
Aged to ashes
And salt
Kindled my child's-heart.

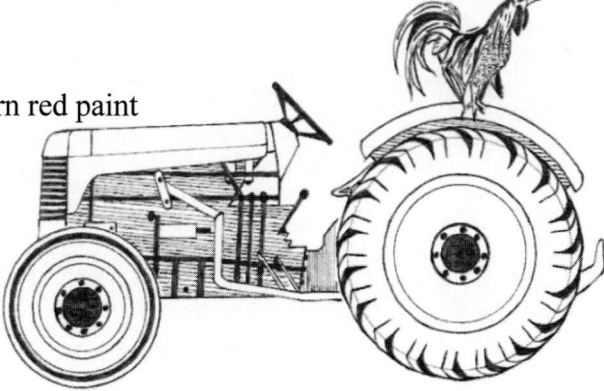

# AUGUST DREAMS

The cows, sublime in daisy-chain,
Go beefing down an August lane,
Swelled with summer clover, grass,
Sweet marigold and meadow.

A boy, behind with weaving dog,
Drags in dreams a stick a'jog
Found broken from a hawthorn hedge.
He nightly homeward follows.

Then through the hawthorn, pale moonbeams
Penetrate his summer dreams
And seal that time in memory
For August dreams tomorrow.

# THE SCENT OF BUTTERFLIES

Spiritual enchanting thing,
Angelic whispering of wing,
What purpose to your fragile day
Where sagging clouds hold sun at bay?
Grey horsemen under clear blue skies,
Amassing, threatening to ride,
Arousing in that insect brain
A sense, the fear of charging rain.
Instinct thin and ultrafine
Cossets gentle life sublime,
Then to feel the weighted splash –
That searing fatal sabre slash.

Fall to earth and wounded lie,
Delicate stricken butterfly,
To rise from mosses soft and warm
And float above that summer storm,
A speck of light of rainbow hue,
An upward flight in fading view,
Between those flashing hooves and blades
Through brilliant sunlight's streaming rays
To a place of clear eternal skies
Filled with the scent of butterflies.

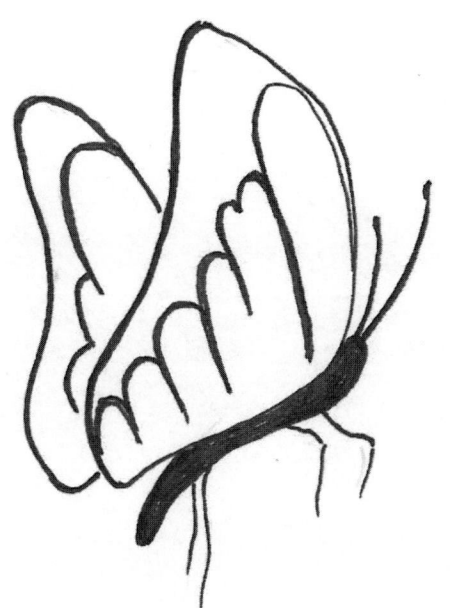

# A SPORTSMAN'S CONSCIENCE

Will I have to face a jury?
Will they all wear looks of fury?
Is human life on a higher plane
Than that of creatures I have slain?
Will the judge be a giant hare
Piercing me with a vengeful stare?
Will the bench be a row of trout
Once tickled with a fatal clout?
God gifted those exquisite things
Taken for this sportsman's whims.
"Thou shalt not kill" said their maker –
I disregarded life's creator.
Defence could claim I killed to eat,
Yet eat I would without that meat.

And then again, who should defend?

This guilty man – stands precondemned.

# WHEN YOU CONSIDER THE ORDINARY FLY

When you consider the ordinary fly
And take its effect upon the cow,
There proves a bovine lack of design
In length of tail from stern to prow.
The elephant, on the other hand,
Is equipped in every way,
With a tail at either end
To keep the flies at bay.
But when considered without the fly,
How blunt these beasts would be!
With neither tail nor nose nor trunk
To sweep the blights away.
Perhaps the fly is not excess
To every creature's needs –
Maybe this pest (for pest it is)
Could somehow be redeemed?
So, when next you consider the ordinary fly
And contemplate its lot,
You may perchance then hesitate
Before you take a hasty swat?

Or … maybe not!

# ONE FOR SORROW

Treading lightly, 'neath a clumsy boot,
He snapped ice blades to pierce dawn mist,
Where the slightest sound reached ears of instinct,
From ground that silent frost had kissed.
Only a persistent mole erupted warmer soil,
Quietly upward with determined will
To penetrate that armoured crust
And tumble down its crumbly hill.
Nearby, a raucous crow, black as its cloak,
Barked from a naked branch,
Its cold breath hung frozen in the air.
Hooded reaper of discharged souls
Beckoned woe from over there.
Alerted, a mountain hare reared upright,
Betrayed by a lingering summer coat,
To run a slalom of wall, gap and fence,
Heart pounding, to hide again
Where winter bracken hunched so dense.
His abandoned doe, petrified,
Crouched motionless to remain at bay,
Until a shout from a distant croft
Raised her pressed ears, and away –
First to right, then to left,
She turned and swerved, no pause for breath,
Then fell,
To gently lay in quiescent death.
Afterwards, as the dawn shroud cleared
To a sharp stilled early morn,
In that silence after the shot
When respectful birdsong is withdrawn,
A cackling magpie swooped
To peck the corpse of a frozen ewe,
His pied mate hopped to join the ghoul
In culinary joy for two.
The gun again was raised to shoot
And left just one - for sorrow.

## ON A SHEEP'S SKULL

There is no wonder
When I stare at you
And see how little
Room for brain,
That such a senseless beast
You were in life.
And though the lower jaw
Is gone,
I wonder now
On what impulse
You did know
To chew.

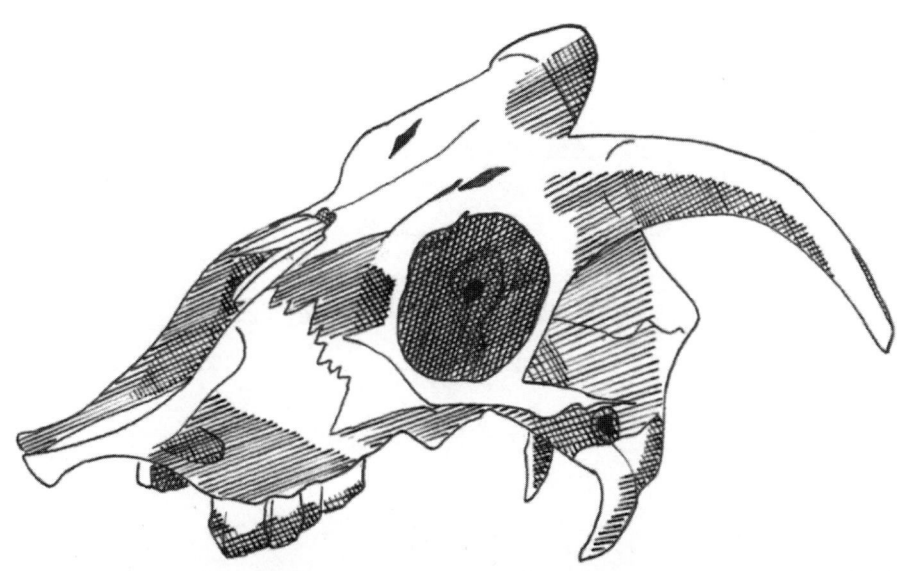

# WINTER BLUES

Were I to try,
I may sleigh
Upon an avalanche of words,
And yet be unable to say
Anything profound.
To skim the surface of reason,
Cutting with ink through deep snow,
I make only temporary lines.
Underneath, the ground lies hard and cold,
Until the soft green beak of spring
Pecks the surface through,
And yet again I try to write of
Inexplicable things,
Wondering,
Why that same force
Breaks through me from time to time,
In some cold-word form.

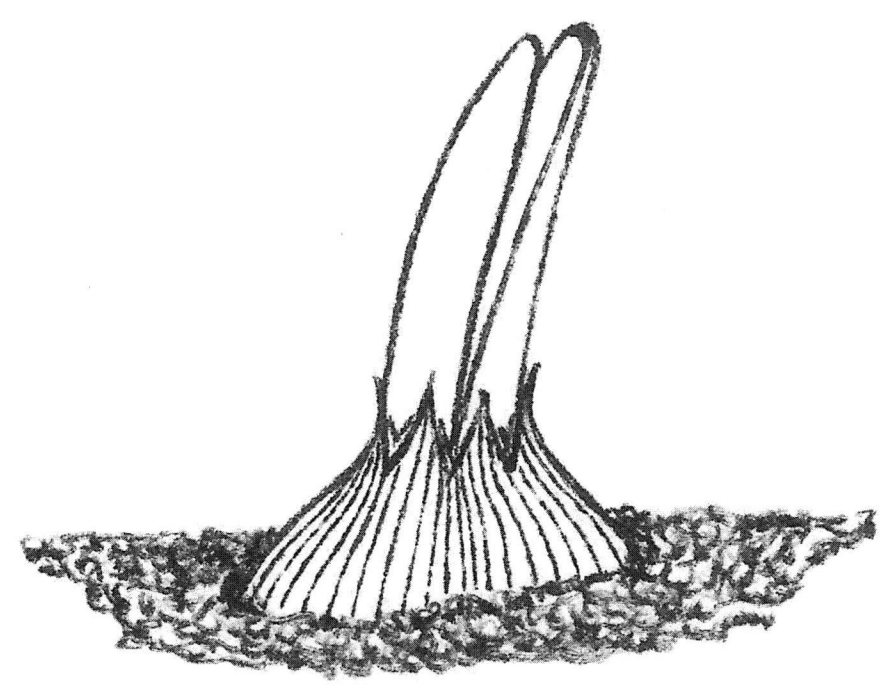

# SHOT

The shot smashed the silence –
Round rubies of blood scattered,
Ruffled, and sank like
Warm ladybirds on snow,
As the echo throbbed back
Like a dead pulse through the mist.

# LAMBHEART

Today life bursts in white lambheart
From pale blue wintershell, and
Easterbirds sing chatterspring
And all God's world is well.

The daffodil in overture
Trumpets 'spring is here' and
Heralding awakes new life
To another summeryear.

# THE KINDER TRESPASSER

Luminary snow light exposed Mister P
as he gingerly stepped through the night's
white topping on the drystone wall.
His feral shape, Manx tail and ear tufts,
merely glimpsed in the camouflage of
summer's scruff,
were now captured, silhouetted and clear
on that bright winter stage –
where a glow from the crouched window
and a bowl of warm milk laid in the snow,
a feline trap
to forever ensnare that vagrant cat
from a life of vermin diet
to the quiet soft nest of a lap.
He was larger than the standard tabby,
lynx-like but smaller,
rag-rug-torn and shabby.
We were never quite sure why he scoffed that bait.
Did we adopt him and determine his fate,
or he adopt us, a milk-life to purrtake?
He chose the role of a domestic cat.
It's just … he never quite looked like that.

*Trippers* was set to music by Phil Hartley, a fellow member of the Irish folk band "Hair of The Dog". They performed it as my birthday surprise during a gig at The Devonshire Arms in Baslow, just outside Chatsworth Park. The relationship between poetry rhythm and lyric writing is in my opinion inseparable (although some poems don't easily transpose into songs).

## TRIPPERS

We love a run to Derbyshire, me and my old lass,
To sit at side o' Fox House Road and picnic on the grass.
Wife and me 'ave a council flat an't garden is a box.
There's now't like that in Derbyshire,
Just miles o'moors and rocks.
On a Sunday if it's fine a lot o'folk get out,
But me an't lass we're used to folks –
To us alt' crowds are now't.
On shifts I work in't foundry,
Stoking up for t'steel,
Me weekend off's but one in three,
And tha can imagine how that feels.
Out here thas left alt' smoke be'ind,
Bar occasional Park Drive tipped.
We like to just relax, unwind,
To get away from't city's grime
And enjoy alt' beauty on its step.
We've been to Monsal, Lathkill and Hope,
And parked on't Winnatts Pass.
There's nowt like a run in Derbyshire
To me and my old lass.
We've seen Little John's grave in Hathersage,
An't sheep dog trials an' all.
Horses jumping at Chatsworth House,
And 'ad a trip round Haddon Hall.
Though we 'aven't got a lot o'brass,
We've saved some year by year,
And when t'work sends me out to grass,
We'll retire to Derbyshire.

Prizewinning poem Derbyshire Festival 1979.

# ODE TO A 1936 MORRIS JENSEN MOTOR CAR

1936 Morris Jensen, good condition, one owner, fifteen quid
And a telephone number I just can't remember.
What on earth's a Morris Jensen?
Dad thought a Morris Eight –
With a short extension.
What better guardian could a youth engage
Than a slow motor car near twice his age?
What restraint, not to show delight,
And swell the price of that gleaming sight.
Her alloy painted coachwork riveted to wood,
Brilliant red, with shabby black hood.
She even had running boards, and the tyres were good.
And then I drove my treasure home,
Straining to contain my glee.
All this, all this, belonged to me,
And all for fifteen quid.
How I fettled her, and how she shone.
Now with badges and mascot on,
We started out, an epic run
From Sheffield to Sheringham.
Our bond grew as youth slipped by,
And oft' I now suppress a sigh,
As whilst canoodling in the back
The chassis broke with a mighty crack!
We abandoned her with heavy hearts
To be towed away and sold for parts.
Unrequited lust,
Now memories from afar
For my first love …

A Morris Jensen motor car.

Continued

Last time I checked, only three Morris Eight Jensen-bodied cars remained in existence, so I thought it was important to keep these photographs of mine for posterity.

## DADDY'S QUOTE FROM HAMLET

"Neither a borrower nor lender be"
Is what my daddy said to me –
"No credit cards you can't afford,
Or mortgages you can't ignore.
Don't window shop a popstar's scene,
Always live within your means –
Look after the pennies,
They'll grow into pounds.
And when I am no longer around,
Remember the words I said to you
And see just how those pennies grew.
Neither a borrower nor lender be,"
Is what my daddy said to me.

Footnote: So why am I always skint?

# NAÏVE

She came down in a negligée –
"Are you sure you want to go horse riding?" she asked.
And I said, "yes."
Must be among life's most serious regrets.
She later became a penthouse pet,
And I, someone she'd forget.
She wanted to dance at Las Vegas,
To sing alongside Elvis,
And I, became married!
She did meet Rod Stewart –
I love his music –
And I'm just deciding …
Whether or not
Rod went horse riding.

Naïve or what!

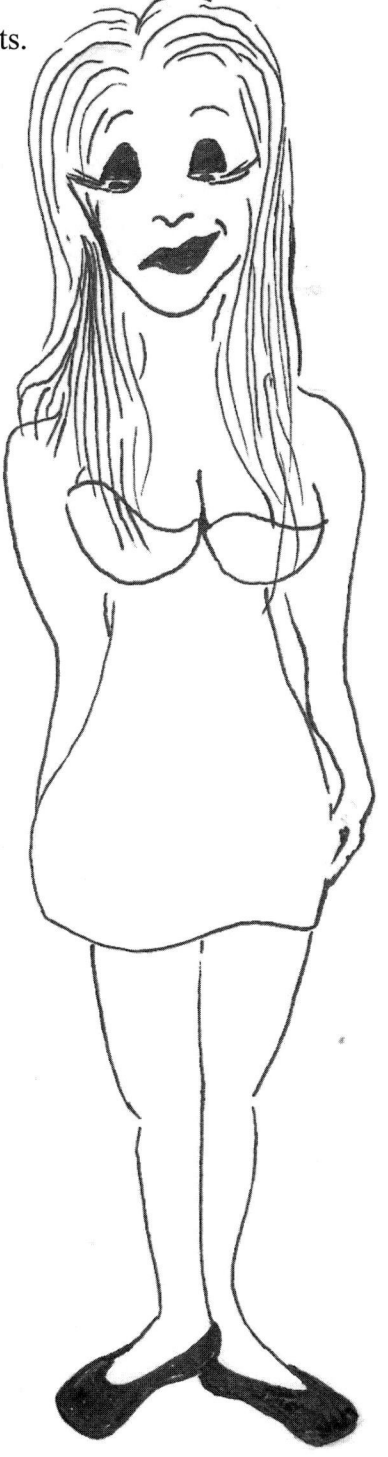

# SANTA'S SPITFIRE

The theme was Santa's Spitfire
With polystyrene wings,
Showroom dressed up brightly,
Lots of streaming things.
Santa in the cockpit
With goggles scarf and hat,
Searchlights turned upon him
To light the tinsel flak.
A young man at his desk
For all who passed to see
Displayed, much like those polished cars,
Beside a Christmas tree.
Across the road, a grocer's shop
With pretty girl assistants,
Some glances passing to and fro,
But they always kept their distance.
There was a dance in Bamford,
The locals all went there,
He wore a velvet jacket,
The girls put up their hair.
Dave Berry sang on dim-lit stage,
Dressed in black with gloves and tie,
His *Crying Game* a top ten hit –
Girls danced together all that night.
Our car salesman (shy? It's true!)
Daren't ask them for a dance,
So propped the bar with other lads
And forfeited his chance.
Next day he glanced across the road,
The cold outside was grave,
Snowflakes fell between them
As he gave the girls a wave.
The gesture passed unnoticed,
Their lives and time moved on,
And the days of Santa's Spitfire,
Had quickly flown
And gone.

Continued

# SWEET PEAS

Sweet Peas remind me
Of the lips of girls –
The Moulin Rouge –
Day-dance, soft kisses of French-pink
In white taffeta
And violet blouses.
Row upon row of Can-Can girls –
Swirls of petticoat lace,
And soft, powder poster-paint.

## DAY-OFF DAYDREAM

A distant tractor shimmers lines
Of shining sweat in upturned soil,
As all the human world but me
Strains collar-tight in toil.
But in my mind there is a vale
Of summer clover sun,
Where insects drone
In meadow grass,
Bumbling with hum,
And cattle chew the timeless cud
Of everlasting day,
When all my boyhood world, hung sweet
With scent of buttercup and hay.

# MATLOCK BATH

Matlock Bath where the Derwent flows,
The town where all the bikers go.
Limestone cliffs, an awesome sight,
Overlooked by Abraham's Heights.
It's like the seaside with no sea –
Fish and chips and mushy peas –
But people seem to like it,
They motor there or bike it,
From all the hum drum towns around,
In Matlock Bath they'll all be found.
Screaming kids and big fat dads –
Ankles smacked, boozed up lads,
Giggling girls out for a laugh,
They'll all be found in Matlock Bath.
On a weekend if it's fine,
Motorbikes are parked in line,
Gangs in leather roam the bars,
No parking space for motorcars.
And cable cars go here and there,
Overhead, for those who dare.
Matlock Bath, the Derbyshire Dales,
Rain or shine, it never fails
To pull the people out in droves.
Forget the sea and sandy coves!

Continued

# SUPER SALESMAN IN THE SEVENTIES

Living well beyond his means,
Worried much more than he seemed,
With the hanging threat
Of the monthly debt –
Met only by commission cheques
As rising costs were unforeseen.

Children then were true dependents,
Unrecognised in a business world,
His wife seemed far less sympathetic,
As precariously her life unfurled.

And just now and then, he asked himself …

Why?

# A GIFT FROM MY COLLEAGUES

It was a chilled, late October half-frosted night,
When breath puffed out and lingered in the still air,
As did the puffing smoke of the oncoming train.
We all waited,
Some huddled or crouched from the cold
As the brute surged towards us,
Huffing and screeching as it lurched to a stand.
Funny how once aboard, the same summer faces
With winter noses,
Appeared from behind mufflers and scarves one by one.
The station seemed eerie and stark
As I glanced from my brightly lit compartment
Towards the British Rail platform clock
Shrouded in mixture of mist and smoke.
How were they to know
I would not be seen again on the 5.45,
Or about my new gold watch
Still in its presentation box?

## DREAM CATCHER

On awakening,
It seemed
My dreams
Were caught in nets,
As sleeping
I had trawled the night's
Dark subconscious depths,
And there they hung
Hard and dry
Like cuttlefish
Against the sky.

# THE CAT SAT ON THE MAT

The cat sat on the mat –
I pondered on that
And wondered,
What this soft and delicate
Creature thought?
Was it content to sit
Preening itself
With sweeping licks,
Wasting the feline day
Thinking of prey,
Or stalking something innocent
To kill and take away?
Returning to softly lay
That offering at my door,
Then later, roll and play.
Those same swift claws
Catching the wool,
And pulling it down
Over my eyes.

*A poem written for Writers in Schools, a project initiated by the Yorkshire Arts Association in the 1970s and 1980s, where writers, including myself, participated.

# FEEDEM, BULL AND DRIVEL, CHRTD SURVYRS, CHRTD AUCTNR, EST AGTS VALS –

Capacious home of character
A wealth of charm and taste,
Dating back to Magna Carta –
    Though the deeds have been misplaced.

Wall and loft insulation
Gas central heating throughout,
A very recent innovation –
    Jacobean no doubt?

Garden, well stocked, easily maintained
With southerly aspect too,
A gloriously unspoiled domain –
    Our totally unbiased point of view.

Double garage to the rear
With up and over doors,
Scribed on each with His and Hers –
    Delightful, need we say more?

A breakfast room sure to delight
Wall-to-wall Artex ceiling,
A setting to raise the appetite –
    Should that decor be appealing.

Well-proportioned dining room
With feature fireplace,
Windows flooding in the light –
    And draught, where it isn't double glazed.

Continued

The lounge being deceptively large
Is ideal for entertaining
With sliding doors to the decking –
    And the scent of open draining.

A cast iron staircase stands
In fine antique design,
That spirals up to the gallery –
    Shutting granny out of mind!

Upstairs, range six large bedrooms
With sweet ensuites in all,
And extensively fitted wardrobes –
    Should the lovely Camilla call.

And should you require to go
As a further aid to the clean,
There's a matching bidet in each loo –
    In subtle aubergine.

I wrote the following poem for a leap-year party in 2008.

## LEAP FROG

*He* an elderly gentleman frog
And renowned great romancer.
*She* a gorgeous, rather exotic
Blond and slinky tad … pole-dancer.
*He* had vast wealth, great lakes and ponds,
Whilst *she* had only a tadpole thong.
*He* was not in the best frog health.
*She* saw her chance for instant wealth –
"Leap year it is – let's quickly elope."

"Too late" – a cry – "Old froggy's croaked."
Too much excitement for one old frog,
Who a tad … pole-dancer tried to rob.

So, if confronted by tad … pole-dancers,
And you're a frog who fancies his chances,
Keep your money deep in the pond,
And steer well clear of
Tad … pole-dancing blondes.

# MICKEY FINN

What spirits lie inside you, cat,
Close to silence now enslaved?
Nagless wives?
Screamless brats?
You may have been –
Politicians.
Nine loud voices,
Bottled,
Shaken,
And poured
Into toxic purr.

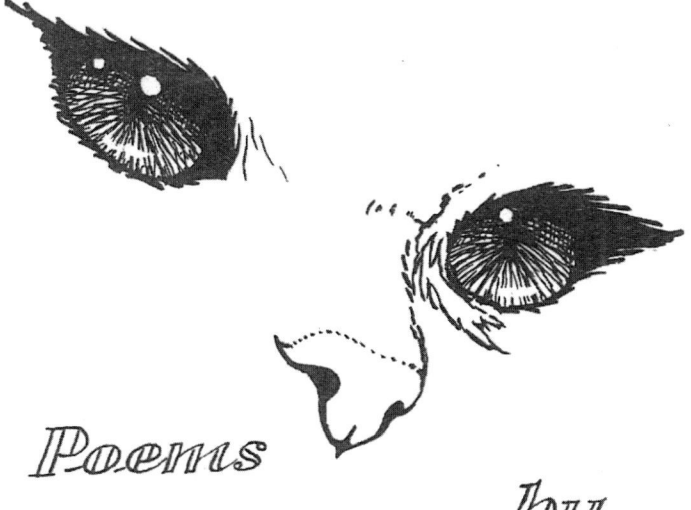

Mickey Finn was the title of my second book, supported by the Yorkshire Arts Association and with an introduction by Alex Boswell, Head of Communication Arts at Sheffield University, 1978.

# SPLIT MAN

He is like Jekyll and Hyde,
A split man,
Poet on the one side
The other a sham.

His mind is like Korea,
A battle.
Between each ear
Machine guns rattle.

# ALBATROSS AFTERNOON

A mist that cooled the frail sun
Hung in the rye grass, clung to spider webs
And numbed the still air.
The colours were of those caught
By an old camera, in snaps
Of highland cattle, standing knee-high
In the shallow Dee.
Summer-birds had gone –
The sky seemed suddenly hushed.
Only the raucous call of a distant crow
Penetrated the mist, so it seemed
To sit on my shoulder;
And I remembered the words
Of a friend, who said
Silence was in me.
If that is so,
The afternoon was mine,
And the crow
My albatross.

# OLD MOTHER HUBBARD

The coroner said,
The cause of death was neglect,
No food in her cupboard,
No warmth in her hand.
Unpaid electricity bills on the shelf
And a final rates demand.
This nation had taken its toll.
Infants, who had heard her plight
In nurseries by candlelight,
Were grown and in control –
With political promises
Of food and warmth,
They greedily bid for power,
Whilst she, embracing her hungry pup,
Succumbed to her needy hour.

# DREAM CAR (JULY 1976)

This week of the announcement of the Rover 3.5,
British Leyland's dream car,
My partner and I
Had one in white and one in brown,
And after work I must confess
I parked at fifteen different pubs,
Hoping on arrival somebody would guess,
Who's this with taste?
Who's this with flair?
Within those tinted windows, he must be debonair.
The radio was tuned to Pop,
Just a jot too loud,
Hoping, without noticing, to attract a crowd.
And as I downed my sixteenth gin,
Aloof within the Grosvenor bar –
Imagining how I'd part the crowd,
Sweep through them in my Supercar –
A girl approached in uniform,
I fancied, to try her luck,
But alas, she came from the Car Hire firm,
And away my keys and dreams she plucked.

Moral: never drink and drive!

# DRUNK

Any drunk can drown
In an inch of brook
Or wine,
Or a fathom of self-pity,
Like that sodden drunk's …
Or mine.

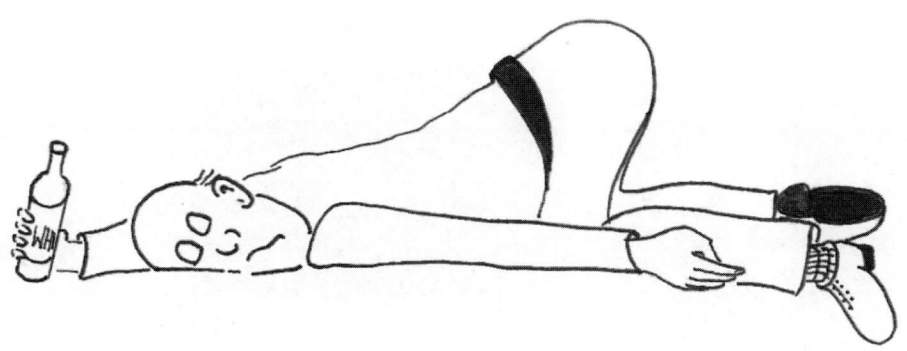

## DELIBERATE RHYME

Deliberate rhyme, I hate it,
But people still create it.
Where every line
Has to rhyme,
And where they can
They make it scan.
Some chosen words
Are just absurd,
But made to fit -
Like the wrong jigsaw bit.
Poetry like that's
Not Sylvia Plath's,
Humour like Pam's
Or John Betjeman's.
'Cos they are fun
And not hum-drum.
No deliberate rhyme,

You'll never find THAT in mine!

## THE NIGHT I DIDN'T WALK OUT

It was like an inverted
Explosion,
Everything blew inwards, and
Even the six hours 'til dawn
Lay punctured on their side.

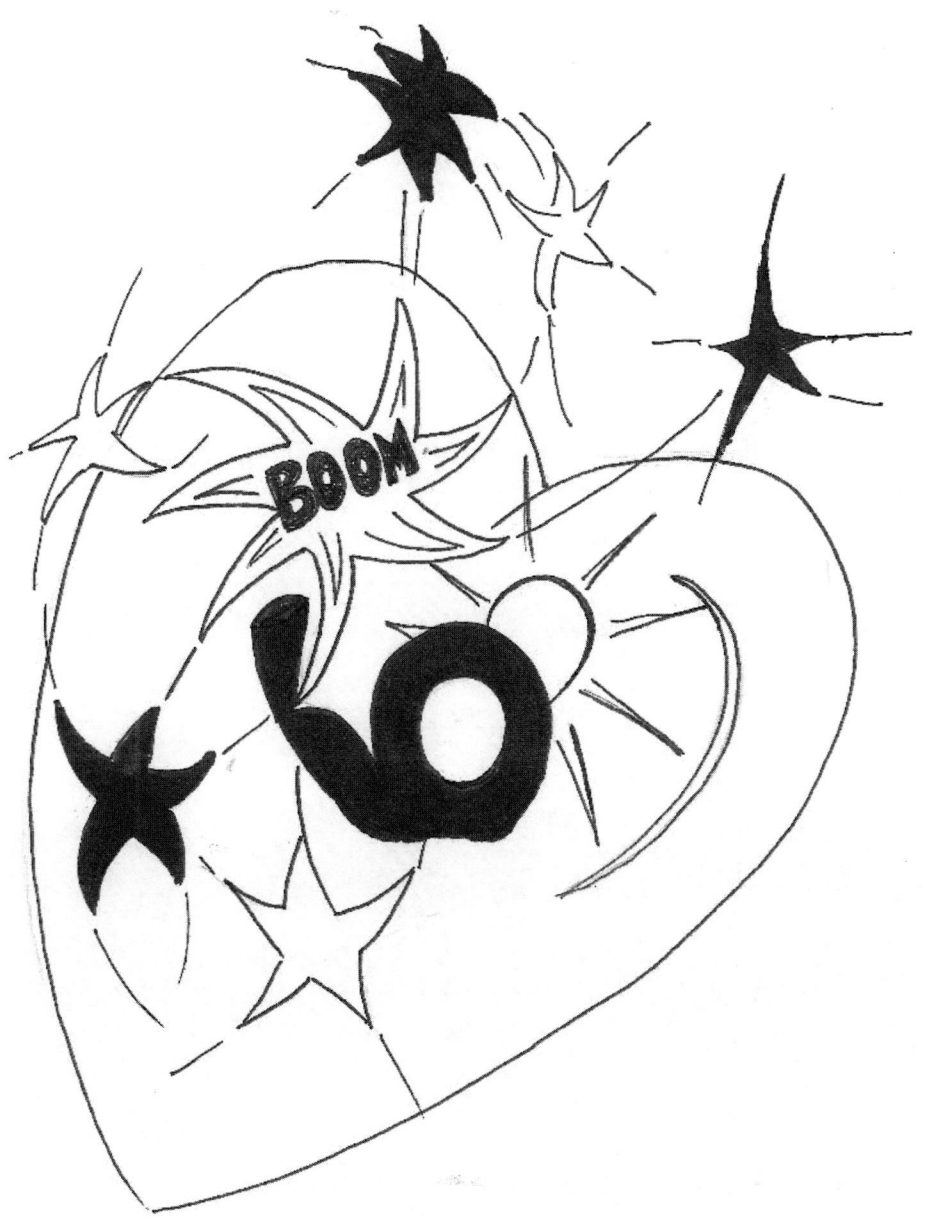

# BUTTERFLIES BATS AND OWLS

*Where do butterflies go by night,*
*And where are owls and bats by day?*

Butterflies cling to cabbage leaves –
Owls sleep hoot-wink in hollow trees –
And bats hang, like umbrellas, in caves.

*But why, when butterflies go to sleep,*
*Do they not fall off?*
*And why do bats and owls*
*Go to sleep by day in*
*Dirty trees*
*And dark old caves?*
*Oh, tell me why – do say.*

My darling, if I tell you all
Of butterflies, bats and owls,
Then still I could not say
Why butterflies sleep under cabbage leaves,
And owls and bats in trees and caves.

*But why…?*

## KITTY'S GARDEN AT CHRISTMAS

If you could but see them clearly,
The hawthorn berries like clustered jewels
Hang ruby-pearled on filigree.
Kitty's garden is framed by trees,
Today, the spruce is bearded white,
The birds seem black.
Starlings, rooks, even a robin turns its back
On an old intruding Ashton cat, trespassing
In Lily's summer domain.
Lily is a cossetted cat, white as the croquet lawn.

Winter garden, soft, snow-cloaked and hibernating –

Kitty can't tend you now –
Wait until spring.

# MAIN STREET

Here, on Main Street, where each family lives
Within holly and goose fat Christmas-houses,
And dogs and cats bulge
With season's bits –
No hungry child-hands reach out
For sustenance,
Just gift-filled eyes
Staring at the TV shows.

Soon we'll prepare so-called surprises,
Love-wrapped, expected desires.
Child-shepherds will watch their parents flock by night –
And smile.

Baubles hang in years on our tree.
A Ford Model T, plastic car, hazes
In the memory of my Christmases,
When it never snowed,
And new yellow whiz-copters and
Humming-things spun in
Disappointing, nearly-snow drizzle.
.

Boxing day was always
Dull relative day, when
Aunties arrived in moth balls
And my knees were
Shining clean with carpet.
Exciting Christmas-eve tree
Was somehow
Finished now –
Better take it far away –
Only to be left spineless
At the top of the garden,
With a few remnants of tinsel hanging –
Reminders of the long months ahead,
Until the TV turns it on again.

# THE REJECTED POET

Deeper than an ocean's base,
Further than the edge of space,
Expression of the deepest soul,
Infinite thought's subconscious hole –
Black, beyond the furthest star,
Only dreams could reach that far.
In wordsearch to express his love
Through unchartered hosts above,
Enlightenment, from other worlds,
Until that symmetry unfurled,
And then he read it as his token,
Lovingly, and softly spoken –
A poem, in heartfelt tones at last.

But she merely tossed her head …
And laughed!

This early fine art print, dated 1863, is by William Powell Frith. The subjects are Alexander Pope and Lady Mary Wortley Montague in *The Rejected Poet*.

## CLOWNING WITH RHYME

How easy it is for critics to say,
"It's depressing stuff you write,
Why can't you write more jest,
Isn't life depressed enough
Without being even more depressed?"

Often, for conversation's sake,
Liberally applied with charm,
They may, in a small-talk kind of way, say,
"Why not try your arm,
And write a book or play?"

As though it were an easy task,
A momentary endeavour
(A second's inspiration)
To scribble out a comic play.
Perhaps they'd like a book an hour,
Twenty-four each day?

In every line a quip of fun,
Mirth in every paragraph,
And like Pam Ayres
They'd have it rhyme –

I'll make you laugh,
I will – next time.

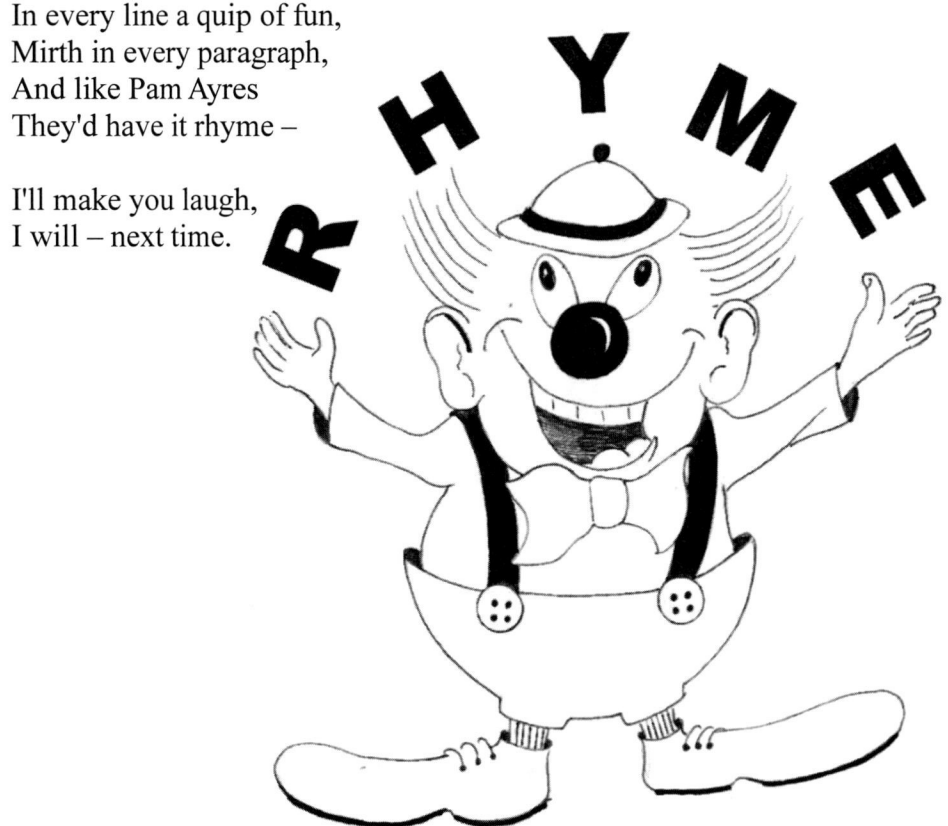

# RAIN ON FROGGATT EDGE

The edge, now, seems newly cleaved,
Bright rain-rock from the lightning strikes,
Where the highest pinnacle, silver shines
Like Camelot's armoured knights.

Beneath, the startled world slows down,
As heavy sheep descend that hill,
Each weighted form bound in wool
And locked in silent terror still.

The gap between the ground and sky
Draws airless as a shallow breath –
Even the cowering birds don't fly
As darkness seems to fall like death.

Halls of heaven open wide,
The lightning strikes again,
And thunder rends the skies apart
And angels fall as rain.

Continued

The rain has stopped now.
The air is new.
And fleeting mist of the angel's wings
Has left the edge in view.

Now in warmth the watery sun
Airs the wings of a dragonfly,
And a thunder stumbled bumble bee
Wipes the storm from its eye.

The sodden sheep line
Steams like a train.
As step by step, each lighter tread,
They trudge to the edge again.

And now the sun like a brand-new God
Unveils its newborn world.
And a lark, as a sudden spirit freed,
It's voice on wing, to that heaven hurls.

# SYMPATHY

Was "It's better to have loved and lost than never to have loved at all"
Not without exception, the most futile remark of all?
And if "There's plenty more fish in the sea",
And if "Time heals", as you say it does,
Then cast your net 'cos they're not for me,
And grant an age to erode my love.

# SCHOOL FRIEND

She saw at once yet did not see,
As I saw her, and she saw me.
I saw at once yet did not see.
And as we passed each other by,
As I passed her, and she passed me,
We glanced towards, then glanced away,
And I saw her, and she saw me,
We saw at once yet did not see.

# HIGH SCHOOL REUNION

It's twenty years, Miss Trott,
Since you terrified
At Dore and Totley High.
As for the reunion,
I am bewildered as to why
I wished to come.
Maybe 34 is an age for nostalgia,
Perhaps I wish to see
If those other privileged ones
Have done as well as me.
You haven't changed, Trott,
For you and your team,
It seems time has stopped.
Not so for us –
One by one,
Those same plain girl faces,
Now hidden under masks
Of forbidden rouge and years,
Reappear, like those rows
Upon the long school photograph.
I've aged like the others,
I suppose,
Though I'd like to think,
Better preserved.
An age of curves
Has blossomed
Between gymslips and now,
When mothers and spinsters
Reassemble
For horrific reunion.

*DORE AND TOTLEY HIGH SCHOOL REUNION*

# AUTUMN TREASURE

Autumn leaves fall off the trees,
They are red, and yellow, and brown.
We like the leaves, one day last week
We saw them falling down.
We walked to the top of Curbar Hill,
And round The Bent to The Fold;
Our lovely walk was triangular,
And we wished the leaves were gold.

# TADDIES

The pond lay heaving in jellymass,
Congealed with primeval forms.
Hatching black yolks,
Jerking into new triggerlife,
Flicking and dangerous.
Pop-eyed, half-cocked,
The taddies hide,
Now log-still, black blobs
Growing wide foetus hands
And prehistoric glands,
To leap
Leg-long
Out of the pond
And crouch frog-eyed
To throb like bombs.

## A STARLESS LAND AFAR

And I could steal a boat tonight
And drift upon the sea –
And I could then forget my love,
And she could forget me.

And I would sail in a star-lit bay
And search for my Shangri-la,
And drift into oblivion,
And a starless land afar.

Inspired by A.A. Milne's *Lines and Squares*

## BEWARE THE BEARS

We may walk the path of life,
Not daring tread to left or right,
Afeared to step on any crack,
No forward leap or stumble back,

So scared the bears will get us.

When we think we should go on,
But terrified to get it wrong,
The dread so deep to take that leap
When all around they softly creep,

We're scared those beasts will eat us.

We must be brave midst snarls and clawing,
Step with care for fear of falling.
Jump those cracks and don't look back,
For courage fends off all attack.

Those bears are so appalling.

Stride now forwardly and sternly,
Feet placed carefully but firmly,
Stand with ease within the squares,
And never, ever …

Feed the bears!

# THE LONG WAY DOWN

I saw the seasons passing,
Someone sweeping leaves,
Heard youthful, raucous laughing
In breeze amidst the trees.
I climbed the highest branches,
So confident my tread,
No backward falling glances,
Within a focused head.
Truly, it was not easy.
Sometimes, tired, I'd stop,
But never looking backwards
For something I had dropped.
The seasons kept on passing,
And when I'd reached the crown,
There was no more sound of laughing.
Just a very …

       Very long way down.

# PERSONAL VIEW OF SHEFFIELD

Opaque dawn mist folded back,
Translucent, as I gazed down over my city.
This moor hadn't changed since
Those bullying centurions hacked
Their way over Stoney Ridge.
Down there, now, things were different.
Gregarious creatures, men, drowsing under
A piecrust of red rooftops.

It's a dogged self-sufficient town.
Founded on the elements,
Shaped by the 'Little Mesters' –
Angular men in cloth caps.
You can see them still
In the Botanical Gardens.
No sweat rags, mind.

The September sun, exhausted,
Cast a disdainful finger
Toward Park Hill flats
That staggered like three tin commandos
On a fun fair rifle range,
Beckoning to be knocked down,
If the Luftwaffe ever came back.

*We* did it though, before they had a chance!

The mist had begrudgingly revealed
A diamond-cut clarity,
A panorama.
They were all awake in the City now,
An indeterminate radio buzz
Shimmered across suburban Dore.

I left, to return that night.
A solitary aircraft above.
Below, the cluster of town lights
Cupped like jewels in a mighty palm.

Continued

# A Little Mester

## MEDITATION ON A NORBERT GOENEUTTE PICTURE

I shall always remember,
My darling Louise,
How I let our lives and love slip by,
That grey afternoon on Boulevard De Clichy,
Chilled beneath a snow-hung sky.
Hansom cabs swished past regardless,
Horses padded through slumbered snow,
Unaware of my sorrow and loss.
Bemused, I watched them go.
The wheels had hewn your tiny footprints –
And you were gone.
I remember drifting home,
Childlike, touching each stark elm,
As together we had once playfully done.
But the trees bloomed then –
As did our love.

# PANNING FOR GOLD

If I keep on writing –
On law of averages
I'm told,
There's exciting
Inspirational
Solid streams of gold.

# RAVENOUS

A raven snatched at the dreams of a poet,
Pulled words in hunger from the head,
Gulped them down for chicks at home
To pacify those bairns unfed.
Expectant beaks raised wide open
Skyward to mother's homeward flight,
A greed for words as yet unspoken
To soundly sleep fulfilled at night.
Bellies full of word-creation,
Quietly they settled sound,
Satisfied, replete and warmed
On softly feathered eiderdown.
As somewhere, a scavenged poet still writes,
In a bird safe roosted haven,
Of cloudless peacefulness tonight –
Out of sight of a sleeping raven.
When a single star of inspiration
Shines from past, yet newly born,
Upon a galaxy of words
As yet untouched, unshaped, unformed.

# SUPERCHARGER

Champions forfeit lance for chance,
Charger for supercharger,
Plumes for fumes,
Spur for blur,
Mace of tournament
For pace
And talisman painted racing cars.
Damsels still bear fluttering hearts
For the brave who flaunt their lives,
With the chivalry of Byzantine knights
And those skills of ancestral pride.
No coat of arms of lord or squire,
Or fights for name or honour,
Just mercenary motives of manufacture,
And a trophy
For the noble winner.

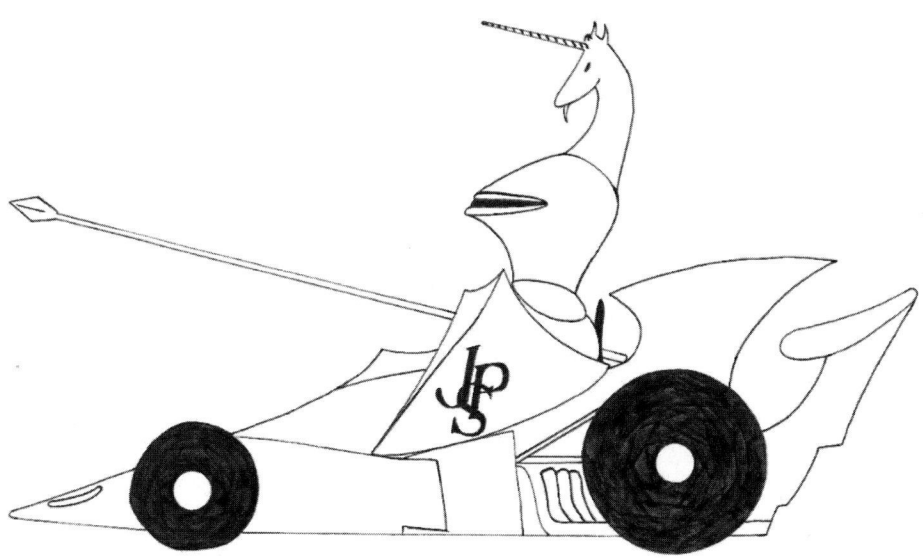

The Lure of Chatsworth?

Sir John Betjeman, UK Poet Laureate from 1972 until his death in 1984, resided from time to time in Broomhill, a leafy suburb of Sheffield, whilst paying regular visits to Lady Elizabeth Cavendish, daughter of the tenth Duke of Devonshire. I couldn't possibly comment on their friendship, but I suspect that it was on one of those visits to nearby Sheffield that he wrote *An Edwardian Sunday, Broomhill, Sheffield*.

I particularly like John Betjeman's poetry, which inspired me to write the following:


## TO JOHN

The mind of John Betjeman
Curled up in dry leaves
Strewn along suburbs
In ankle high breeze,
Where a passing school bus
Filled with girls from 'The High'
From Broomhill to Fulwood
Twice daily sweeps by,
Taking giggles and secrets
To bedrooms indoors
Where discarded creased uniforms
Lay untidy on floors,
And wilful young ladies
Downstairs do descend
In conspired steps to freedom
Every weekend.

# DIVORCE

Law cuts through years
Like a surgeon's knife,
Separating
Man from wife.
Anaesthetized,
Severed love,
No mops to wipe
Congealing blood.
Relationship
Pronounced dead,
Instruments
Shining red.
Prostrate bodies
Numbed by pain,
Staring backwardly
In vain.

# THE RIFT

When anger vengefully builds a rift
Over which spans a rickety bridge,
The bravest dare not cross.
And beneath, in a stream of venom cold,
Runs stricken love as the years flow
To a bitter sea of apathy,
Where only serpents breed,
And a sadness
Off their milk doth feed.

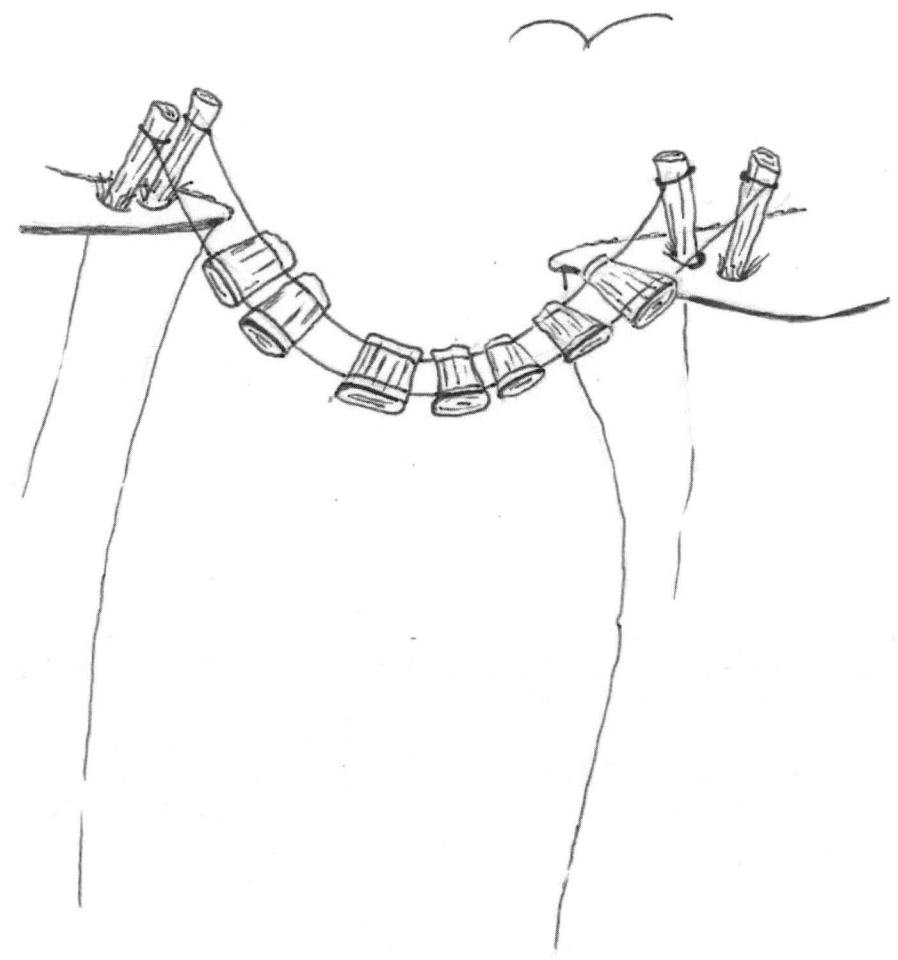

# CHESHIRE CATS

Cheshire cats
In fun
Make pokes
Pointed claws
Whiskered jokes.
Crouched behind
Feline grins
Moggie smirkers
Know something.
They'll never tell
Do not fear
Purring smiles
Ear to ear.
Lips rimmed tight
Teeth glow white
Secret's safe
Sleep sound tonight.
Tomorrow
They may disappear
Leaving
Just a knowing
Sneer.

# HIVE

His toil was like a bumble bee's
Gathering nectar anxiously
From flowers of fragile life.
A pollentaker from the hive –
That place the lazy empress sat
As others worked
And she grew fat.
Heavenhive of golden honey
Clear blue skies, fragrant rich
Warm and bright and sunny,
And he, just like a faithful drone
Flew to and from the honeyhome
Amidst those golden rays –
And that is how his beelife was
Those work long busy days.

## SIMON SAYS

Simon says my poetry's good –
Simon says, Simon says.
So if it's so good,
So good as Simon says –
I can't wait to add
To the verse I've written,
To impress Simon
Who's obviously smitten.

Just off the A621, between the Sheffield outskirts of Owler Bar and the village of Baslow in the Derbyshire Dales, is a second left turn that takes you over the moors towards Chesterfield. Just after that left turn, to the right of you, lies Leash Fen, an unmarked boggy area of unkempt moorland, but once an ancient settlement.

I wrote *Leash Fen* first as a poem. Later, it was put to music. Sometime in the early 2000s, I joined an active Irish folk music band called Hare of The Dog, but some three years later, split away with one of the other band members to form the duo Deliverance, with me on banjo and my duo partner on guitar. I imagined the song being sung by the wonderful Kate Bush. But no, just us! We did perform *Leash Fen* at various venues, and I can clearly recall one such venue being The Trout – a pub in the village of Barlow, near Chesterfield, just down the road from Leash Fen.

Continued

# LEASH FEN

When Chesterfield was heath and broom,
Leash Fen was a market town.
Now Leash Fen is heath and broom,
And Chesterfield's a market town.
And that is how the legend goes,
The lost town on the moors
Where ancient people dwelled
Twixt Whibbersley Cross an' Sheffield.
'Tis mystery why they left or died,
Deep inside Leash Fen they hide,
Wi' bits o'pots, remnants o' fire,
Wisps of ghosts within the mire.
Those primitive and hardy things,
Far beneath the swamp they bring
Faint memories of life,
So softly where that moorland lies.
Leash Fen a town upon the moors,
Long since devoured by rain,
Is visible through depths of mind
And risen once again.
Dimly now across the time
No noise they make, they quietly smile.
"I cannot harm you – I am here.
You're so frail – do not fear!"
Just as quickly did they fade
Mist beneath the everglade.
Now Leash Fen is heath and broom
And Chesterfield's a market town.

# SEAVIEW

In a thousand years from now
A man may stand just here,
And see the things that I see
And hear the things I hear.
And the sea will keep on rolling
And the sky may still be grey,
But there'll never be another me
Or a day just like today.

# JUST FOR YOURSELF

You're only a skeleton
Covered in skin,
Clothed on the outside,
Exposed on the in –
More or less the same structure
As everyone else,
So what makes me love you
Just for yourself?


Written for Elaine.

# SID THE TRIANGULAR MOLE

Many thousand years ago,
A triangular mole called Sid
Came out of his hole near old Cairo
To build a pyramid.
Muscular, he wasn't
And all they had was sand,
But millions of triangular moles
Popped up to lend a hand.
Sid then formed four great teams,
Each to build a side,
Graduating inwards
With no cement or ties.
Sid, a triangular mole, maybe –
But not of average status.
He held an engineer's degree
And devised the plan in stages.
When the job was done,
The teams of moles went underground,
And from that day to this,
'Sid and Co' have not been found.
The fattest pharaoh at the time –
His name, Two Ton Carmoon –
He liked the 'sheikh' design
 ("I'll have it fitted for my tomb").
But he hadn't got the money,
So first he went to Dad,
And then he went to Mummy:
"Like your last idea – it stinks,
I gave you £15 last week for that useless sphinx!".
"Mummy, Mummy, please stay calm,
I'm not trying to take advantages."

… As he chucked on some embalming fluid
And wrapped her up in bandages.

Continued

# Sid The Triangular Mole

# SERUPTENATIOUSLY

Some poets write poetry
Oh so grand
That no-one truly
Understands.
But those who see
Deep hidden meanings
Lay claim to be
More enlightened beings –
Whereas the hailed writer
Could just be doolally
Or the poetry and verse
May just be wrote badly.
I like to write poetry
You can understand,
Seruptenatiously
By my fair hand.
And I like to make it
Rhyme and scan,
With metre and rhythm
Carefully planned.
Not remotely like that
Abstract guff –
Just Seruptenatiously
Simple stuff.
Take for example,
Damien Hirst.
Dead animals as art –
Is it good, bad or worse?
But some peer knowingly
Over half-specs,
Aficionados, straining their necks.
So tell me please,
Am I missing out here
Seruptenatiously
Something sincere?

Continued

Or like the Emperor's clothes,
Do they just *want* to see
Not a naked old royal
Or pretentious poetry?
"But isn't it grand!
Isn't it fine!
Look at the cut,
The style, the line!"
It's guffappreciatingly
Seruptenatiously
All together
*So* sublime.

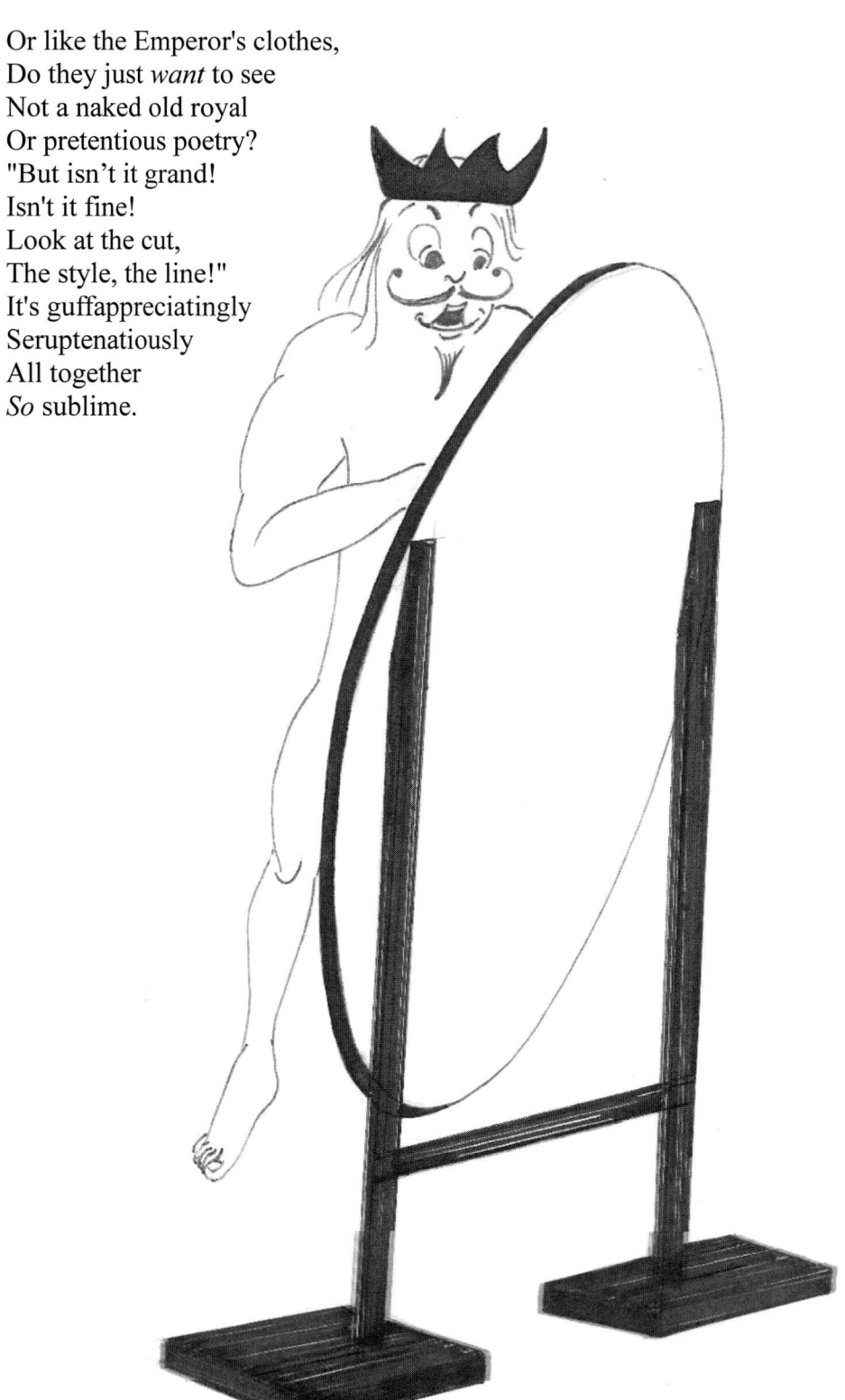

# DREAMERS

We imagine anything -
Make it real –
Mould a dream
To touch and feel,
Make it happen,
Maybe it does?
But not for everyone –
Only us!

"CHADWICK, STOP DREAMING, LAD!"

Why my teacher called me Chadwick I shall never know. Perhaps he confused me with another pupil. Who knows? Anyway, his demand didn't work. I never did stop dreaming.

# IN TWO MINDS

Like two competing brothers,
Equally loving and hating each other,
They lived together inside one brain –
A tumultuous pair wearing two faces,
Outwardly looking exactly the same.

Often trying to understand
The impulse making those demands,
It was an enormous strain –
Hiding a secret no one must know,
Imprisoned within that confined frame.

Sharing a guilt no others could see,
Locked in a mind without a key,
Handcuffed together on life's death row –
Constantly finding new reasons to lie,
Their silence must with them grow old
And with their tumult die.

# GULLS

A squadron of gulls
Soars high in the sky,
Mission complete
They return to the sea
In close formation flight.
"Leader to wing" is called,
One by one they dive,
And skim the surf
In endless search,
Each plunders to survive.
They've flown behind ploughmen,
Ridden the wake,
Scoured flotsam and jetsam
Brought in by the waves.
They scramble with tides,
Then descend from the skies
In relentless patrols
With screeching cries.
And just like those spirits of the sea,
They'll swoop throughout eternity
To raid at will.
'Til, search fulfilled,
Their tortured souls set free.

## SHERINGHAM HOLIDAYS

The Emery's shed now history,
Boats crafted for a century,
Wooden crab-boats built to last
Float now beneath the seas of past.
Those spindrift days like sifts of sand
Slipped quickly through my ageing hands
In grains of faded memory
Of when I was a boy.

A beach hut on the Eastern Prom',
Deckchairs hired to take the sun,
Ghosts that in my mind still chat
Earnestly of this and that,
And some decide to take a dip
Rubber hats and costume strip,
In grains of faded memory
Of when I was a boy.

Now where I stand near this arcade,
No threat the Germans will invade,
Unless perhaps by Charabang –
Mum and Dad and small Wolfgang.
All the guns have gone away
(Remnants of those days affray)
In grains of faded memory
Of when I was a boy.

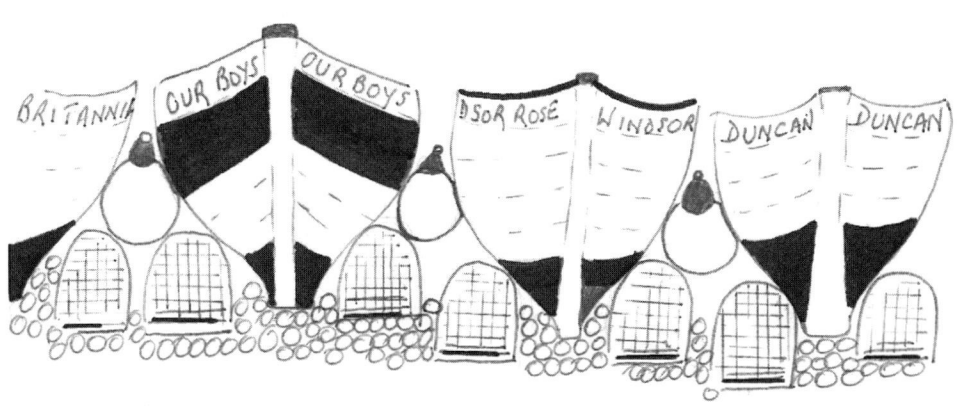

# INK

The black sap
Is desert dry,
Emptiness skims a surface blown
To scratch his vacant eye.
Blinded with searing apathy,
Pushing an arid mind,
Scouring that vast spaciousness
And dragging a tired brain behind.
He trudges the torrid landscape,
Where thirst hangs dog-tongued
                From the mouth,
Licking for moisture in the sand –
Or an oasis in that relentless drought.

## "FRESHCO PROFITS DOWN"

"Freshco profits down".
It's hard to force a frown –
Did they give a diddly-squat
When they came to town,
And all those little retail shops
Systematically lost pounds?
One by one, familiarity
Was replaced by sundry charities,
And mediocrity spread around.
Freshco – the giant disparity,
With all the fears that giants bring.
But just like old Goliath,
          They should remember …

It's the little folk that hold the sling.

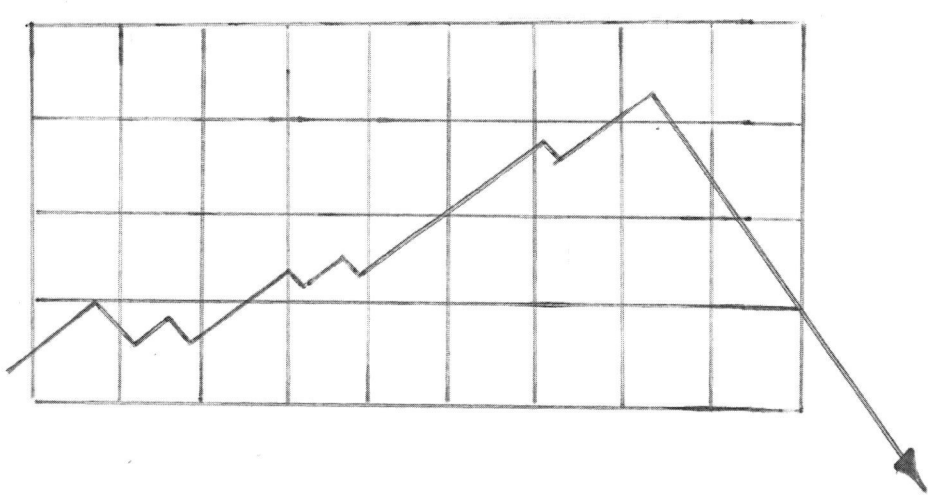

# I TRIED NOT TO BE RUDE

I wrote a letter to the government
About the soaring price of food
And escalating heating bills –
I tried not to be rude.

Last week my wife and I went out –
Our anniversary celebration.
She said, "Take me somewhere expensive, darling,"
So I took her to the filling station.
They say it's nought to do with tax –
It's the rising cost of crude
And the worldwide fiscal market –
I tried not to be rude.

I bet those energy company chiefs
Buy boats off the Florida Keys
And sun themselves all winter,
Whilst the rest of us bloomin' freeze.
And the bankers still take bonuses
For debts that they've accrued,
When public money bailed them out –
I tried not to be rude.

I paid for my "OA Pension"
All my working life –
Awarded mine at sixty-five,
But then they robbed my wife!
All of our retirement plans,
To which I now allude,
Were put on hold 'til we're too old –
I tried not to be rude.

Even funeral costs are rising –
Can't afford the cost of living,
Can't afford the cost of dying.
No one seems to listen.
Hope I won't be misconstrued –
I've really had it up to here
But ….
I tried not to be rude.                    Continued

In the years 1995 and 2011, the government introduced pension changes to equalise eligibility for men and women. This, in itself, sounded fair. But the changes had a particularly harsh impact on many women born in the 1950s. The numerous women affected were on the threshold of receiving State Pension, and had possibly planned their retirement, when, without much (or any) formal notification, they faced a further six years' wait before becoming eligible.

*I Tried Not to be Rude* was published by the Daily Mail in 2012. WASPI (Women Against State Pension Inequality) continue to address this issue of unfairness.

# TWISTER

We are nothing more than dust,
Spiralling towards the ground,
And the twister's crooked finger
Somehow taps out time.
The chaos of our brittle minds
Settles without trace –
And, this being the case,
I shall seek my paradise.
For this twister
Is no respecter
Of the time it taps.

# DRESS SHOP

A masochistic
Endurance in life
Was a day out shopping
With my wife –
In the dress shop
I would stand
Whilst cobwebs formed
On me in strands.
"Does my butt
Look big in this?"
"Is this tight
Upon my hips?"
A woman's spree
Is not a man thing –
Please give us patience
And understanding!

# WONDERGULL INCARNATION

A courtship
Which would otherwise be dull
Is performed
Mid-air by the gull.
With flight skills genetically
They swoop energetically
To express their dexterity in full.
On the cliff
There's a bobbing of heads,
No falling
Or vertigo dreads.
There is nothing appalling,
Just screeching and calling,
Engrossed and enthralling
They weds.
A honeymoon
Spent by the sea
On the roof
Of a fine B & B.
Consummation complete,
Clearly seen from the street,
Is most indiscreet –
C'est la vie!
Pregnancy
Paternally planned,
They maternally
Seek somewhere to land,
To await on a ledge
The arrival of eggs
Amidst those stick-legs
In the sand.

Continued

Soon after
A short incubation,
Miracles appear
In manifestation
Of chicks in a batch,
Which amazingly hatch
And instinctively
Re-enact …

That wondergull incarnation.

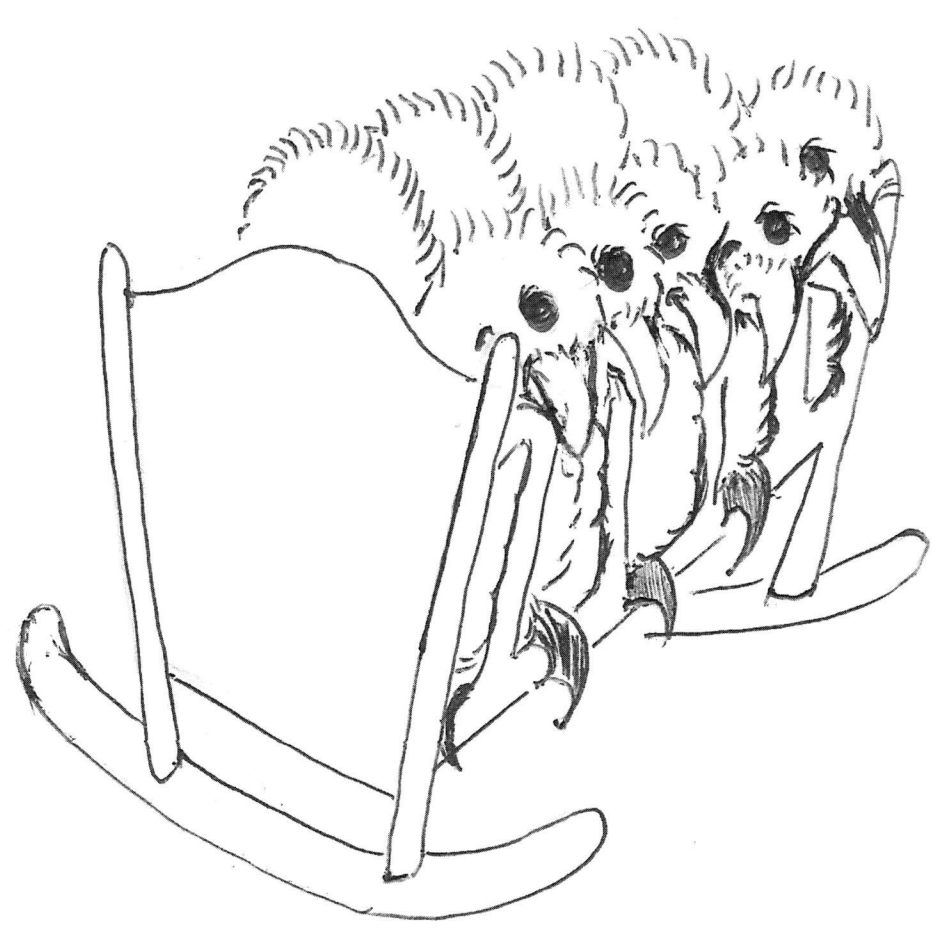

## ODE TO A BOTTLE OF RED WINE or A NIGHT ON THE PISTE

Well, it seems,
With some surprise
I'm still alive –
Having skied
Down the Matterhorn
At enormous speed
And halfway
Up the other side.
Just when I thought
That I was safe,
I started to slide –
Backwards, and
At terrifying pace.
But again,
Surprisingly,
I did not die.
And then I turned over
In my sleep
And skied right off the edge,
Leaning forward
In perfect form and flight,
Not unlike a human kite,
Soaring …
No broken bones
Just a dig in the ribs
For totally innocent
And unconscious
Snoring.
She went
Straight back to sleep
(How does she do that?)
Now with my feet
Firmly back on the ground
And reluctantly
Wide awake,
I could yet
Be more annoying …

Continued

In the middle of the night
I switch on the light
And begin to scribble
This poem.

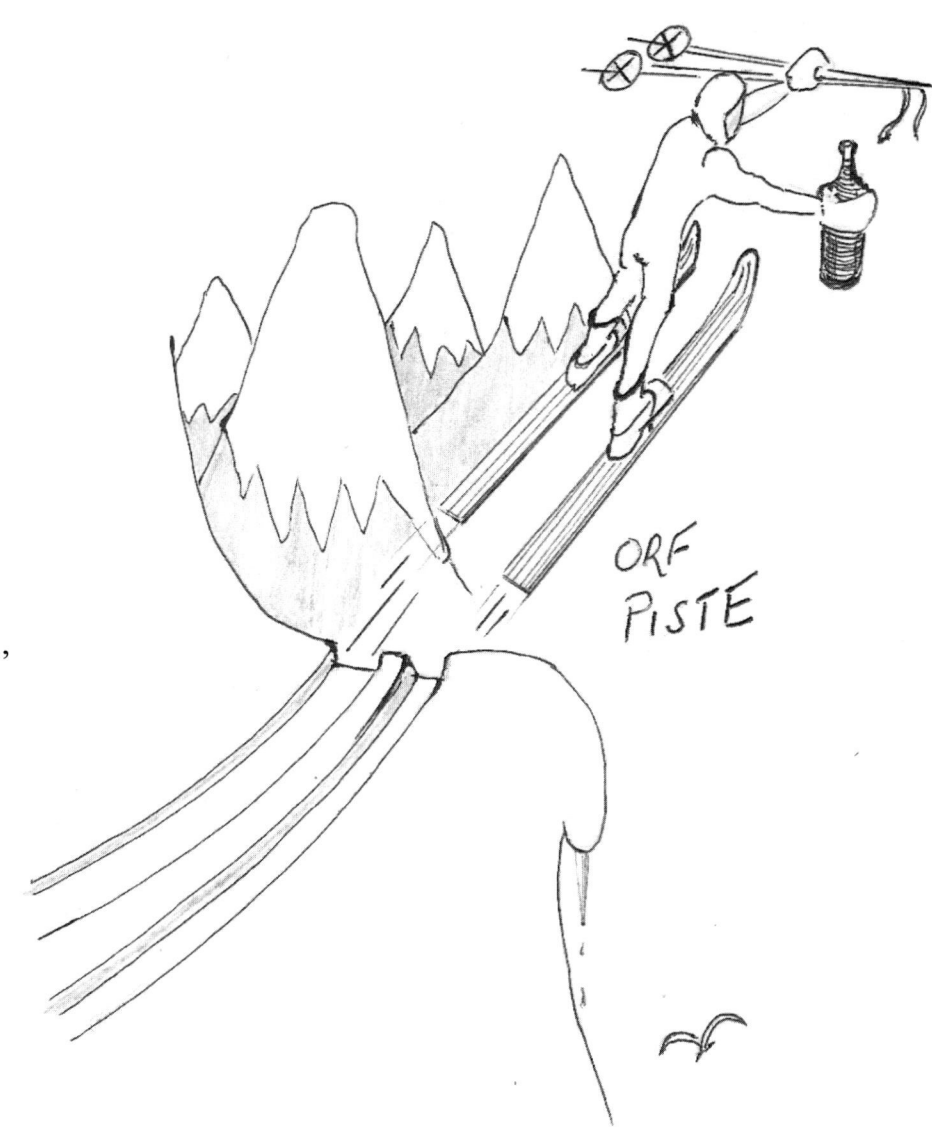

## THE OTHER SIDE

The grass is but a mirage,
The oasis a bowl of dust.
The shimmering lake
From which he slakes
An obsessive burning lust
Is a desert,
Where men leave footprints
In an ever-drifting sand,
Vanishing,
To appear again
On that beguiling land.
As the wind sweeps over the surface
Casts of a Legion are seen
Marching toward that mirage –

Where the grass seems ever green.

# GUYS

"Come on guys,
Do as you're told"
Is now the extent
Of parental control.
And the guys proceed
To do as they please –
And the parents
Oblivious, like absentees.
And off the guys go,
From place to place,
Wreaking havoc and
Mayhem.

Such disgrace!

## ALL SAINTS' CHURCH (BEESTON REGIS, NORFOLK)

Beeston Church was ordained to be reclaimed.
I recall as a boy what that meant to me,
That great North Sea
Threatening, like the Norsemen at Lindisfarne,
To batter the door of Christianity.
And I imagined then, when I became a man,
Beeston Church would be long gone –
Its Norman flint lying like an unanswered prayer
On the beach.
But this was not to be.
Only a few feet of cliff had disappeared
In my long years of absence.
An era may yet pass
Until the white toes
Of John William Craske
Stumble in sleep to the shore,
And his shapeless bones like driftwood
Lay at rest no more.
A desecration by Aegir's hand,
Ever clawing precious land,
From where headstones will hurtle down
To beyond those fragile wrecks that hide like crabs in sand.
And one by one, each forgotten soul
Will fall into eternity.

## UNCLE SAM

So hand in hand
With Uncle Sam
We'll march to the oompah band,
Little Nephew
At his side
Keeping pace
With mighty strides
In search of the tiddlyompom land,
Where the *Star-Spangled Banner* is sung
And the stars and stripes are hung
And cheerleaders prance at the front
In a spectacle
Oh so grand!

# MR EMERY (SHERINGHAM)

There's always been excitable children with buckets,
Scouring for crabs at low tide,
Carefully turning large white flints
In chalky pools aside.
There's always been ladies in 'decks' on the prom',
Resembling my old Auntie Ive,
In large floral dresses by beach huts in August –
Incongruous dames beside the seaside.
There's always been Salvation Army's brass band
Playing on Sundays in town,
And pensioners quietly remembering friends
In tweeded caps cast down.
There's always been crab boats in red, white and blue,
Men's lives in the hands of Our Lord,
To return on the rise of a North Sea wave,
Laden with lobster and crab aboard.
There's always been gift shops with crockery and glass,
Furniture and books in array,
And imported items for profit bought in
To whisk your holiday savings away.
There was always our friend Mr Emery,
Hiring his beach huts and chairs,
Fondly remembered by adults with buckets,
But sadly he's no longer there.

# MAN BENCH

I sometimes get trapped
Traipsing round shops.

*Oh look*, she says, *Darling,*
*Can we please stop?*
*And on the way back,*
*Do we go past ...?*

I try to ignore the place
She named last –
It's a ten-mile detour
But my fate is cast!

Quietly, she chunters,
*We've nothing else to do.*

I think – only think mind you –
"Speak for yourself!"

But then obediently
Join the queue
Of silent husbands
On the brink.
Shopaholics,
Weakest Link!
There's even a bench
For the likes of me.
We sit and wait
So patiently.

Why can't she just go in,
Buy what she wants,
And out again?

To me there's no
Degree or measure
In shopping
Merely for pleasure!

Some say that bluegrass was introduced by banjo pickers like Earl Scruggs, Don Reno, Bobby Thompson and many others with similar styles. But maybe not …

## THE GIFT

The Holy Ghost played mandolin,
The Father played a fiddle.
The Son, he played an old banjo,
Standing in the middle.
Saint Peter played a fine guitar,
As always to the right,
Far left stood Paul on double bass –
They made a holy sight.
And all the angels gathered round
In heavenly accord,
For a spiritual hoedown
Led by our good Lord.
Ghostly fingers crossed the strings
Of a silver mandolin,
A bow of gold in the father's hold
Caressed the violin.
And in the middle stood our Lord
With a banjo in the lead.
And they played with grace
And they picked with speed,
A wondrous band indeed.
And a new and vibrant sound was born –
Their fingers moved so fast –
That night they cast a mortal's gift
And they christened it "bluegrass".

I wrote *The Gift* for a friend, Clem Vickery, who was banjo player for the George Mitchell Minstrels on stage and TV in the late 1970s. He performed his own solo musical speciality act on the show and is remembered as one of the best banjo players in the world.

This poem was set to music and recorded. It was also published in *BMG*, the oldest music publication in the world.

# EBB AND FLOW

For every wave that flows
Back and forth on rocks.
For every tick that goes
Predictably to tock.
We somehow are mesmerized –
Deaf, dumb, and tongue-tied
With other more important things
That life's priorities can bring.
We miss the constant ebb and flow
The tides that daily come and go.
Nothing alarms us to the time,
Other people quietly dying.
But not us – we just go on
Cos we're deaf
And don't hear the gong.
Suddenly it's gone
And then we see
The long
Umbilical life-line rope,
In diminishing kaleidoscope.
Colourfully looking back
Like a joke –
A sick knock-knock-who's-there,
And another clock strikes somewhere.

# 30 DEGREES AROO

Dan was a boxing kangaroo,
A sparring act in an outback zoo.
But every time he skipped or hopped,
He'd turn 30 degrees and stop.
Predictable – you could say that's true,
But Dan did more in a single hop
Than most kangaroos in two.
Quick with limb
And slick with brain,
Boxing was his road to fame.
So armed with gloves
And boxing shorts,
He quickly rose in the kangaroos' sport.
His nimble footwork
And lightning brain
Earned him a very apt nickname.
Inspired by his legendary hero,
He emulated his style,
Worked the gym both day and night
Till toil became worthwhile.

Continued

Unknown as Danny Kangar,
Now "30 Degrees Aroo",
He too became a legend
To the likes of me and you.
He could fly like a butterfly,
Sting like a bee.
No longer predictable Dan,
But a fully-fledged, 30 degree
Heavyweight knockout kan'.
He totally confused his opponent,
You could say
They were caught on one leg,
They'd weave and they'd dive
And they'd parry,
They'd dance and they'd slide
And they'd duck.
But just as they fell off balance,
He'd weald a mighty left hook.
His technique could never be beaten,
His punches could never be blocked,
For every time he skipped or hopped,
He'd turn 30 degrees and ... WHAAP !

# PUDDLE HAPPY

When I was a boy,
Puddle happy and splash free,
Flowers dripped bees
And honey glazed trees,
Thunder blitzed the skies
But didn't bother me.
I lived in a hive,
A sheltered Innisfree,
Where I glimpsed reality
But always scurried back
In time for tea.
And just as a mouse approaches its bait,
Equally knowing, and not knowing its fate,
I gradually, timidly
And very, very cautiously
Sniffed at that reality,
But always scurried back
In time for tea.

Continued

As I grew older,
And age made me bolder,
I took that bait quite willingly.
Some flowers had died
Whilst I was blind
With youthful gluttony.
But then, the seasons
Ran without reason,
The trees and the flowers
No time to have bees on.
And I, entrapped within my cage,
Stared helplessly back
To those Innisfree days.

But now in advancing age,
Somehow freed from my trap
(That infernal cage),
Time has yet slowed down again,
To see fresh flowers
And feel the rain,
As puddle happy and splash free,
I skip toward my Innisfree.

# AUTHOR'S NOTE

## MY CONNECTION WITH CHARLES STUART CALVERLEY

I was not named after this significant Victorian poet. In fact, I doubt my parents and family were ever aware of his existence. It was only by complete chance, whilst exploring a second-hand bookshop sometime in the 1980s, that I was drawn to his collection of poetry, *The Works of Charles Stuart Calverley*. I purchased the book, and as I read the introduction, it became clear that CSC was one of my ancestors. The book referred to Walter Calverley, the family villain, and the story of his ferocious deeds leading him to be pressed to death in York Castle in the year 1605. The events leading to his demise were preserved in the pages of *A Yorkshire Tragedy*, one of the spurious plays originally attributed to Shakespeare and included in some of the earliest editions of his works. At the time of becoming aware of CSC, I had already been writing poetry for over ten years and had, with the encouragement of Enid Hattersley, former Mayor of Sheffield and supporter of the Yorkshire Arts Association, had my first three short books of poetry published.

I particularly like Charles Stuart Calverley's poem, *Love*, which, in my opinion, illustrates his wonderful mischief, wit and satire. But his following poem, *Cuckoo*, was raided by me, cuckoo-like, to make a springtime contribution to my regular poetry column. I made a few changes, for relevance to springtime, but in doing so sacrificed some of its original satire. The following version is our combined effort.

Charles Stuart Calverley's works can be found online. There is a plaque dedicated to CSC on the wall of Cambridge University, where he was admitted to Christ's College in 1852.

*A Yorkshire Tragedy*, has since also been attributed to Thomas Middleton, a successful English Jacobean playwright and poet born 1580. Shakespeare and Middleton both lived at the time of Walter Calverley's death, and again, details can be found online.

Continued

CHARLES STUART CALVERLEY

Continued

# THE CUCKOO

Forth I wandered, years ago,
When the summer sun was low
And the forest all aglow
        With its light.
'Twas a day of cloudless skies,
When the trout neglect to rise,
And in vain the angler sighs
        For a bite.

The sound "cuckoo" piped away
Over cowslip fields of May,
And upon that hazy day
        Seemed to float.
His voice fading in due course,
Maybe just a little hoarse?
And appeared to me to force
        Certain notes.

As that summer passed so soon,
Being toward the end of June,
He, then singing out of tune –
        Not at best!
Without further strident tones,
Took flight for his winter home
Of white beaches, far he'd flown
        For a rest.

Left behind, his ruthless hatch
Had ousted the rival batch,
Whose parents had grown attached –
        To that thing!
Whilst our un-paternal ward
Only cared for vocal chords,
Craving a return applause.
        Wait 'til spring!

Continued

To sum up:

The cuckoo turns up in the UK just as our weather improves, hives off its kids for someone else to bring up, then clears off again for some winter sunshine. What a life!

Remember when John Lennon compared his fame to that of Jesus? Many took offence, but I'm sure it was not meant in a derogatory way. The Beatles were deservedly world famous by then and the comment was quite typical of John's flippant humour. My following poem was written after the very sad loss of both John and George, two of the fab' four.

J.L. - 2008

Who'd 'av thought it –
Now I'm sixty-four
Two 'v Beatles are no more.
So I'm sendin' this to heaven,
He's so famous, that John Lennon.
Imagine this – no address.
No Penny Lane or Abbey Road,
Just care of God, and son JC:
More famous initials …

I'm sure JL would agree!

153

# GHOST TOAST

I approached a ghost
In the middle of the night,
Armed with only
A sharp breadknife.
I asked, in a semi-state of fright,
"Would you like to be
Thick or thinly sliced?"
It quickly turned
And then it spluttered,
"Slice me thick
And evenly buttered!"

# IMAGINARY FRIEND

(To a younger wife)

I wished you were with me when I was five,
But you weren't alive.
I wished you were with me when I was ten –
You weren't alive then!
You could have been there when I was alone,
Enjoying the things I did as a boy –
You were absent again!
I wanted to share (and imagined I may)
The things I did those days.
I never knew
My imaginary friend,
But the friend I imagined
Was you!

## "WHO, ME?"

It's not that I mind should you guess who I am,
You possibly could – I'm sure that you can!
It's just that I wasn't sure whether you'd tell
Or not, and then I thought what the hell!
I really don't mind the thought that you may,
And don't give a damn for what people may say,
But as it's a Valentine Card that I write,
I think that you ought, yes, I think that you might,
Keep it a secret, who it is that I am …
I think that you should – perhaps you can?

# IN BETWEEN

It's between being awake and asleep
They creep into the room,
And just when you thought it a dream,
You wake, and in between
The dream and awake,
They escape again.
It's not to say they hadn't been,
But it's just that space in between
Asleep and awake
When they creep in
And escape again.

A concrete poem

## ROBINSON CRUSOE

R C
WAS
NOT
ALWAYS
AC
DC
WELL
ANYWAY
CERTAINLY
NOT
BEFORE
FRIDAY

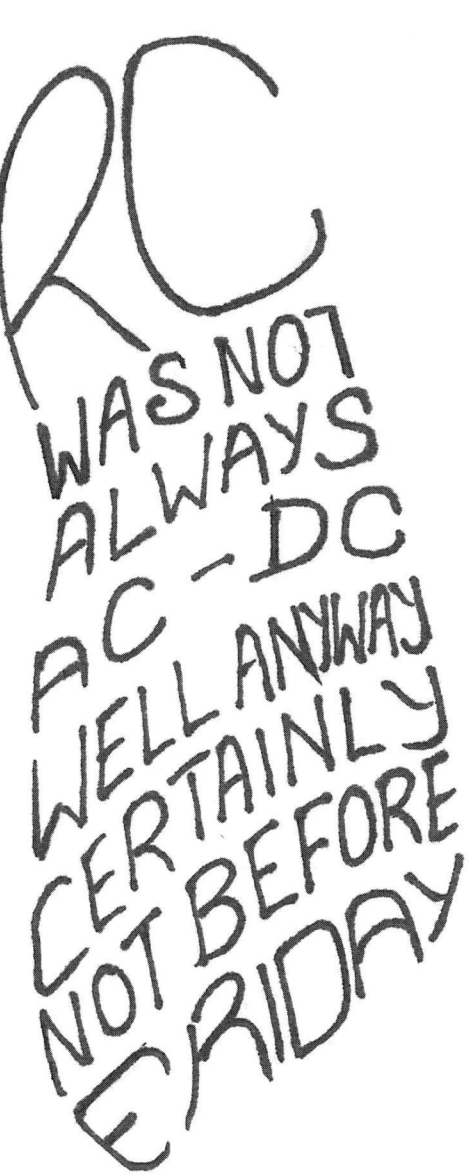

Footnote (Please excuse the pun):

I would just like to make it clear that in this instance RC refers to Robinson
Crusoe and not Richard Crabtree.

# REAPER

Don't come here, my palest friend,
This mortal soul to apprehend.
Pension, savings, cash in hand,
I have retirement fully planned,
Walking health-wise twice a day
To keep the likes of you at bay.
And whilst I loved my dad and mum,
I'd like to have some senior fun.
Although I know they miss me so,
The reunion date – I'll let you know!
I see your black cape drifting by,
Intrepidly I breathe a sigh.
And though I wish no others harm,
Your fading shape brings quiet calm.
A while to reflect on many things
Til time your gruesome coming brings.
When next I see your faceless mask
I may have run life's winding path.
You will have taken other lives
Before I feel that fateful scythe.

# PAIR OF SHOES
## <u>Volume Two</u> (Well, you all know volume one!).

There was an old woman who lived in a shoe,
Who loved an old man who lived in one too.
She lived in the left, he lived in the right,
Both crept out in the midst of the night –
Kissed and canoodled until the dawn,
Returned to their shoes the very next morn.
She slept in the toe, he slept in the heel,
Each of them knew how the other did feel.
Hers was a brown shoe – a battered old brogue,
His shoe was black and really in vogue.
Putting their differences firmly aside,
The old woman schemed to be a new bride.
She worked all day – he caught up on sleep.
Out of her shoe she'd quietly creep.
With paint and a brush and a fair bit of flair,
She gradually made 'em look like a pair,
And then put aside all of her fears
(This was her chance – it was a leap year).
At last came the night – Feb' twenty-ninth –
Clock struck twelve, right on time.
Both crept out in the midst of the night,
She from the left and he from the right.
But time had run out, it couldn't be worse.
Her chance had gone – it was March the first!
So after a night of kissing and canoodling,
They both returned to their own shoe-dwelling.
But this wily old woman, she wouldn't give in
And moved next door to live in sin.
The tale was turned from near disaster
As "the pair" lived happily ever after.

# AWAITING THE WAVES

We watch as grandchildren
Run to the sea,
No parents to call
My sister and me.
Everything seems
Like our yesterday.
Except for those
Time washed away.
And soon the tide
Will wipe the scene,
As it has so often
In between,
When our memories
Will be breached,
Like the castle
We made,
Today on the beach –
Left awaiting
The waves.

## SPRING LOVE

Within the death of winter's hold,
Springtime's birth begins from cold.
And as we die, or love grows old –
Like ours, new loves and lives unfold.

# DNA PART ONE

Deoxyribonucleic acid
Is nigh impossible to say,
And that is why they simplify
Those words to DNA.
It provides the scientific path
To identify our kin,
Our very own ancestral past
From whence we all begin.
A descending and ascending line,
Back and forth from age to age.
The one genetic certainty
By means of D.N.A.

# DNA. PART TWO

When they dug up old Richard the Third,
Removing his skelly from resting.
He was ceremoniously uninterred
And sent to the lab' for testing.
They confirmed his right royal bones,
D.N.A. traced a living descendant –
Who may have been seated upon our throne
If the Plantagenet line hadn't ended.

# DNA PART THREE

So, with the aid of imaginary DNA,
On the track of the rich and famous,
I'm scouring back through my own ancestry
Of forebears down the ages.
But whilst I'm busily doing that,
I can tell you something for fact –
Somewhere out there in the past
Was a living breathing heathen
Without whom
You'd not be reading …
This!

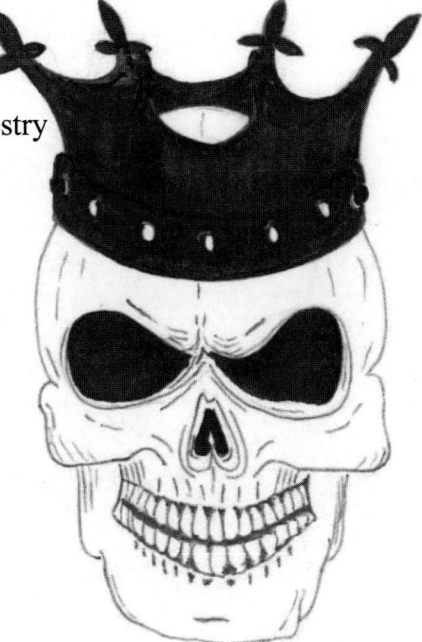

# DUST TO DUST

Here I lay
A ghost in skin,
Old on the outside
Young on the in.
A shell full of memories
Ready to hatch,
The ghost going forward,
The flesh going back.
And the shell, lying motionless –
No more than a crust –
Turns ashes to ashes,
Dust to dust.

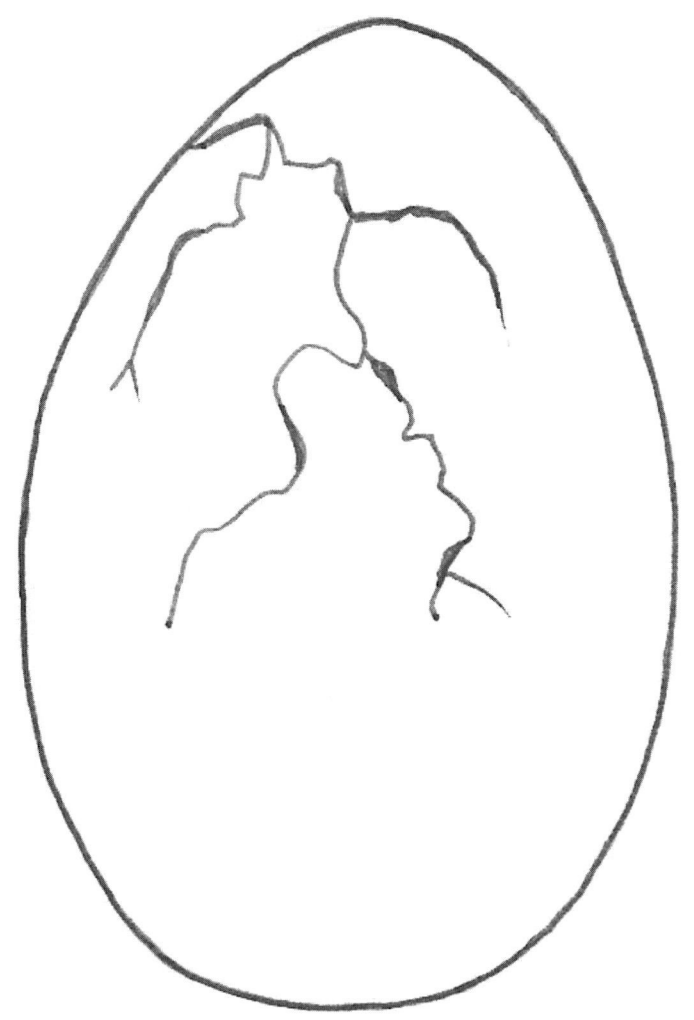

# THISTLE

Thistle, you are lovelier than any English rose.
Purple – bright Scot,
You have in your heart no gentility.
Your scent is that of the free soul of Caledonia.
It is of Eagle's flight,
Atlantic mist,
And memory –
Colourful as Culloden,
Brave as Bannockburn,
This proud head does not stoop like a rose,
Barbaric warrior you are –
In gentle repose.

Footnote:

Although I did not write this poem with political intent, it was passed to the Scottish National Party by Alex Salmond (First Minister for Scotland) prior to the 'No Vote' for independence in 2014.

# FREED AGAIN

Thoughts that may flutter
On butterfly wings,
Or rest on a flower
To ponder on things,
Then hover a while
As dragonflies do,
Or sit on a hill
And gaze back at the view,
A landscape of words
As yet unsaid,
Just a glimmer of something
Faint in the Head.

Then freed again –
A broken spell
By the fairy wand
Of a Tinkerbell,
To write in the depth
And light of a glade,
Stardust sprinkled
On the page,
Those fragile wings
In the inner-ear,
Now ringing rhythms,
Bluebell clear.

## POPPY

One day you'd be queen
Of a wonderful land,
With castles of coral
And acres of sand.
We'd surf on seahorses
And hunt silver fish
Served sweetly by mermaids
On a turtle shell dish.
Or sometimes we'd sit there
And stare at the sea,
And you'd just be Poppy
And I'd just be me.

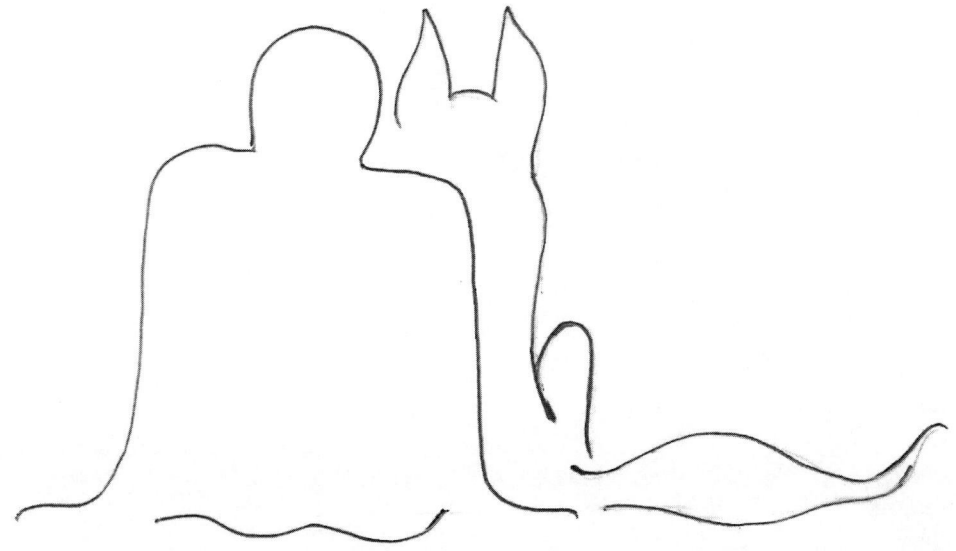

# FOOTPRINTS IN SNOW

As snowflakes
Are formed
In intricate patterns on the window,
Slowly melting into changing shapes
Held by delicate strands,
We link hands and dance,
Leaving tiny footprints in snow,
As our lives step out their paces
On that crisp white floor.

We tread but fleeting traces,
As our love clings to the pane
And trickles softly to rain.

I wrote the following poem having watched a certain celebrity on TV. She is known for having had a "little help". But if it makes you look that good – bring it on! This poem was published in the *Daily Mail* in 2015.

## A LITTLE HELP

The lady'd like a little help
In staving off advancing years,
Some minor tucks beneath the chins,
A nip or two behind the ears.

So, sparing no expense
To rectify those things,
Her quest, restoring confidence,
Intrepidly begins.

Commencing with the surgeon's knife
(Which makes one's knees go weak),
Incisions round the lower jowls,
And down beside the cheeks.

The face is lifted from the skull,
Moved upward just a tiny jot,
Then stitched back with a gentle pull
And tied off with a knot.

Some liposuction here and there
To pipe away the blubber,
Slimming the buttocks, waist and thighs
(Enough to make one shudder).

Continued

Then neatly wrapped from head to toe,
Just like an embalmed mummy,
With G-cup boobs from a former op'
And a gastric bypassed tummy.

She staggers out with sunshine specs,
Homeward from the docs,
But when those bandages come off,
She'll flaunt a size-8 frock.

Her follow-up's just six weeks on,
To take away the stitches
And check for any minor flaws
Or detrimental hitches.

A touch of Botox to smooth the brow?
A waxing to remove some hair?
Then she'll be sorted, more or less,
With those final tweaks of aftercare.

Of course, there'll be orthodontic work,
Half-a-dozen crowns or more,
The promise of a celebrity smile
Admirers will adore.

And so, until the years roll by
To a future time's unrest –
She will, for a while at least,
Flaunt that smile in a size-8 dress.

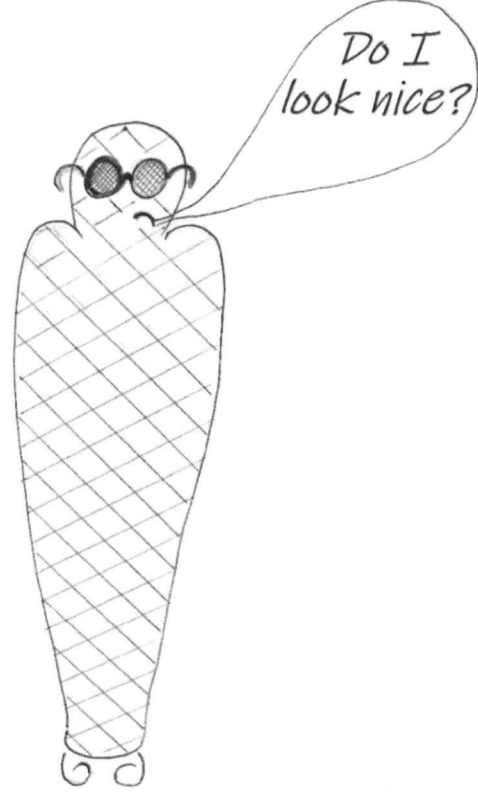

## PONGIDAE GENUS

I'm not now, under any misconception about me –
I'm a monkey!
Not unlike those in the zoo,
And whilst deliberating on a former delusion,
I'm sorry to say, that you are too.
We preen ourselves in a similar way –
Metaphorically speaking we pick at the ticks,
We don't bounce our wrists on the ground
That is true,
But we are suspiciously like ape,
Depending of course on your own point of view.

Pongidae genus, that's me –
Clothed to hide my identity.

# THE GOORONG

High in his castle
In the Derbyshire Peaks,
There dwelled an ancient Goorong.
He lived with his wife
Who always was right,
Whereas he
Couldn't help but go wrong.
He tried his best,
As most fellas do,
To be right
And not to be wrong.
But in the words of his wife,
"He's never right –
That's why I named him Goorong".
Now it seemed so absurd
How she spread the word
And how quickly
The nickname caught on.
It was clear in the eyes
Of nearly all wives,
Their husbands were also Goorongs.

Reply:

For as hard as we try,
And I speak for all guys,
We cannot do right but do wrong.
And so, I suppose,
We accept it from those
Who in all things
Are right … never wrong!

Signed … A very patient Goorong.

# FORGOTTEN

Michael Palin,
Whilst journeying in Tibet,
Was told by a Buddhist monk
He'd just met,
That he'd been an elephant
In a former life.
To which Michael didn't,
But should have replied –
(Allow for a brief pause in the chat)

"An elephant, eh!
You'd think I would have
Remembered that."

# BIG BROTHER

Someone a mite smarter than me
Invented my brand-new Smart TV.
It's so good-looking, sleek and slim,
Electronic brainpower programmed in.
Does it ever switch off its interface,
Or continually feed via cyber space?
Maybe it listens to all that is said,
Filling me with fear and dread.
Even unplugged it's watching me,
Whilst chatting over a cup of tea,
Waiting for that Freudian slip,
Careless words between each sip.
A demographic spy installation
Gathering data throughout the nation,
Linked directly to the web,
WW dot nosey neb.
The question is, does it actually think –
Reporting how much booze I drink?
Having opinions, of one sort or another –
A telltale working undercover?
The cardboard box was innocuous enough,
Plain black lettering on buff –
How was I to know any other?
That I may have let in a covert
Big brother.

# HIGHWAYMEN

If Turpin were alive today
And saw the changes we have made,
He'd be a child in a grown-up world
Of spaceflight jets and motorways.
Earth to moon in several days,
Around the globe in under nine,
Dickie's eyebrow may have raised
At London to York in four hours' time.
Hijackers since have hit the news
And terrorists are our latest threat,
Gone are those days of carriage and hoof,
The 'gentlemen' in black, in silhouette.

# LIKES AND DISLIKES

There are people I don't like
And people who don't like me,

I don't know why we like or dislike
Or why this oddity seems to be,

We don't have to meet,
We don't have to speak,

I can't explain
This anomaly,

But I know who I like, and who I dislike,
And I know who doesn't like me.

It was a cold, clear Christmas Eve in the year 2016. The time was approaching midnight, and I was walking my dog, Poppy. The moon was a silvery white, and the clouds were unusually formed in wispy lines. There was one bright star to the right-hand side of the moon. The finishing touch, I thought, would be for Santa to be riding a sleigh with the full team of reindeer across the night sky. And then I thought how Christmas had changed in my lifetime.

## AND THE REINDEER REST IN LAPLAND

The moon is a Christmas snowball
Over upturned slush on high,

Where delivery vans rut tyre marks
As tinsel clouds float by,

And tomorrow's glee below
Lies calm in sleepy eyes,

Whilst headlights glow like moonbeams,
As eBay's little helpers drive.

And a single on-line star
Shines down from ever changing skies

## SCARRED FEET

Now I can see clearly at last,
Walk straight through opaque past,
Tread in my father's footsteps
Over shards of broken glass.
And limping just in front of me
The man he wanted me to be –
Almost … but regrettably
With scarred feet.

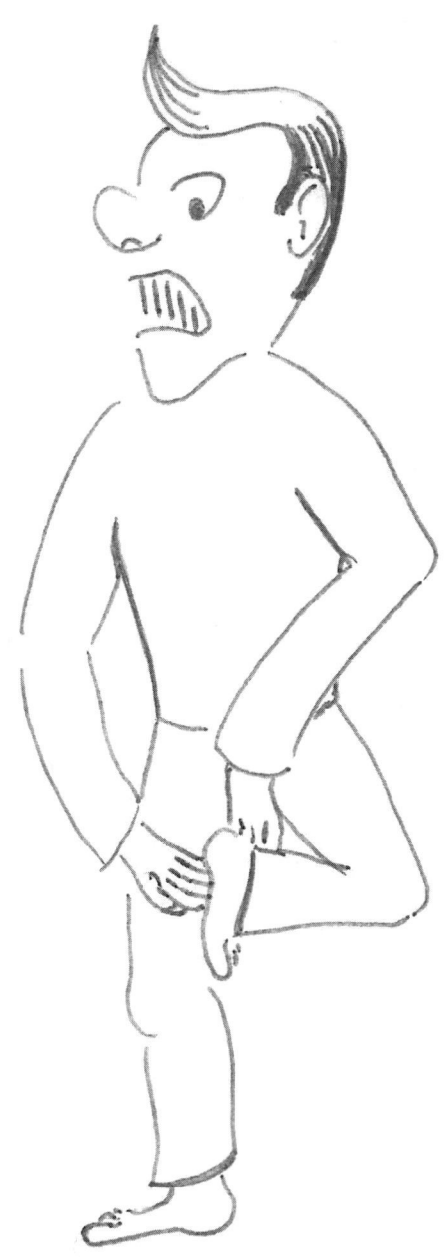

## ONION

His mind was like an onion
Peeled back from a hardened outer skin
To many layers of tears and joy concentrically within.

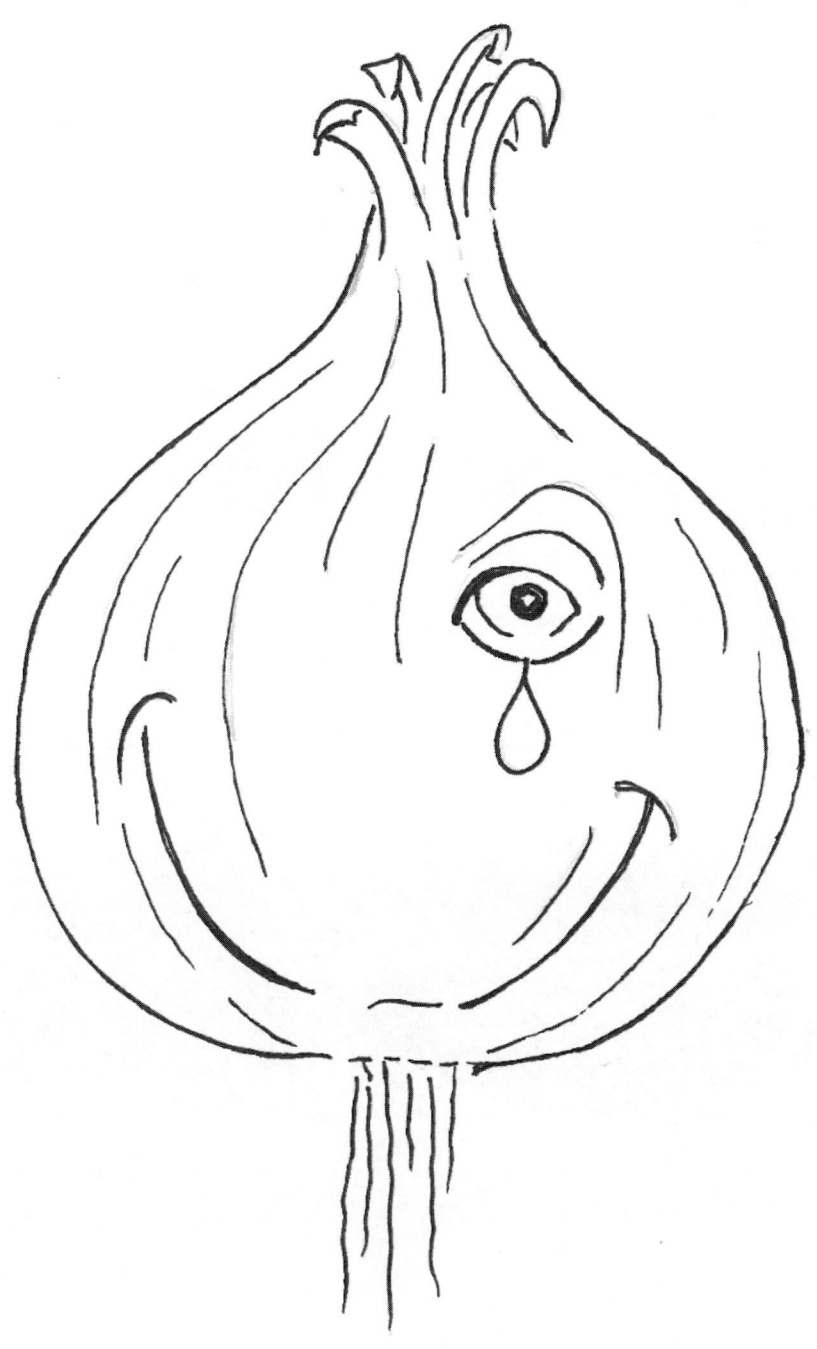

## I'D MURDER FOR A BURGER

Are we primitives armed with clubs
That we still eat bludgeoned meat –
Can you taste the pulsating beat
Of the beast
You would not have the heart to kill
If it were a pet?

During the 1920s, Sheffield was held in the grip of gang warfare. The most famous gang was the Mooney gang, led by George Mooney.

My grandfather was a Chief Detective Inspector at the time, based in Sheffield City centre. This was long before the introduction of the Panda car, and the horse was the fastest mode of transport. My grandfather and other police officers often had to gallop from West Bar to West Street, where trouble was rife (to say the least of it).

In the 1930s, my grandfather retired to Edale, in the High Peak of Derbyshire, with his trusty police horse, Loch, where he resumed the more peaceful work of his forefathers – farming. First at The Orchard, then Waterside Farm and lastly at Ladybooth. It wasn't until after the war, and my grandparents' deaths, that my own father returned to Edale. That's where I came in.

I wrote the following poem, which later became a song entitled *Take me back*, which tells of my family's close association with Edale since the 1930s. The song was performed in 2006 by yours truly (as one half of the duo, Deliverance) as part of the opening celebrations for the state-of-the-art Visitor Centre in Edale.

I had returned to the village after several years' absence, and it seemed both strange and emotional to be back, singing and playing my song, opposite the church where my parents and several friends are laid to rest.

# TAKE ME BACK

I think of those long summer days,
When we all toiled to bring in the hay.
The sound of the curlew
And lapwing o'rhead flew,
It all seems a long way away.

The old folk they dwelled in the Dale,
Their voices I hear to this day.
They were happy with friends there,
I remember their laughter,
As afterwork card games were played.

When Grandad first came to the Dale,
They'd only just brought in the rail.
He'd retired from The Force
With Loch, his old horse,
All the Mooneys were banged up in jail.

It seems such a short while ago
That I pulled many fish from the Noe.
I roamed upon Kinder,
The time didn't linger,
Now I wearily wend my way home.

Take me back to the valley I know,
Where from boyhood to man I did grow.
And the hills rose so steeply,
The birds sang so sweetly,
And quickly my river did flow.

The song was also runner-up in a national lyric-writing competition.

A soul or not a soul ? That is the question !

Some exalted scientists have rejected the existence of a soul. Others, by contrast, have stated that far too many unanswered questions remain to doubt it.

Religion of many denominations throughout the recorded history of mankind believe in the existence of a soul.

I have always been curious as to why some children can be unbelievably talented at an age where, by every law of reason, they ought not to be – if only by virtue of the time it takes for normal progress to reach those levels of excellence. Some artists could practise for several lifetimes and still not reach those levels. Or that is how it seems.

Anyway, whether you believe or not is a wholly personal thing, and that is why I had to write my following poem in the first person.

## RESIDENT

I took up residence in '45
In a body my parents sought to provide.
I could not recall then, from where I'd arrived,
But from that point forward, I was alive –
Or at least my body was.
First, taking for granted those bodily things
Of sight, sound and mind,
Touch, desire, movement of limbs
In almost too perfect design.
I did later, from time to time,
Looking metaphorically from the inside out
And the outside inward again –
A spiritual act of major contortions –
Consider the human form
To be functional, peculiar,
And wonderful,
In almost equal proportions.

Continued

midst that confine
I knew myself,
Impulses I could not help,
And the inner part I played
Pondered why it was that way.
Throughout the tenancy I grew,
But hidden traits, *I* only knew,
Facets which made me as I am
Remained deep-seated in the man.
My body aged, so too my mind –
As the contract term drew slowly by.
Whil'st trapped inside those ageing limbs,
Dwelled this youthful soul within.
Looking back upon my life,
I recall, on behalf of self (as in 'body'),
And incumbent former wife.
We too played host
To two former ghosts –
Or at least our children did.
And now I approach a familiar door
I sense I've passed through long before,
To take my turn in silent queue
In a place obscured from mortal view.
With no past sight or sound to call on,
Just enlightened shadows of the foregone –
I wait …
To be cast upon a life unborn
In a brand-new contract,
As yet
Undrawn.

# THE INVISIBLE POTION

Instinct and souls
Were stirred in a bowl
And poured into origin's ear,
A whisper of –
"Now you are on your own"
Could be heard as that potion cleared,
And a promise –
"The one who believes in me
Will live even though they die"
(But between now and then
When we shall meet again –
Use the instinct and souls as supplied)

## THE GREED

Greed ignores the Arctic thaws
As snowflakes melt on swollen seas.
Sounds of deafening silence roar –
Rainclouds weep on fallen trees.
Above, glare former living stars,
Where other peoples failed to see
The greed within those worlds afar
And where that hunger leads.
Yet we, in depths of disregard
Abuse our fragile world,
Defecate on our own backyard,
A foulness round the planet swirls.
Population grows and groans,
As human swarms consume the earth.
Scant public crowd-control is shown
Or unity for nature's worth.
The birds and beasts once save by Noah
Are sacrificed by driven greed,
As hands grasp out for more and more
To satisfy inherent need.
And when the recklessness is done,
Our damaged world forever changed,
What once was recreational sun
Will spread unplayful flames.
Oceans will rise in floods of tears,
Dowsing all selfish desires,
As we're drowned in our stupidity,
Fingers burned, playing with fire.
And as the deserts and oceans grow,
A panic will arise to flee,
The greed no consequence by then,
But far too late for you and me!
When *this star* will glow in the universe,
A desolate warning of our deeds.
The beacon of inhumanity
And our failure to stop the greed.

## SLEEPLESS IN SHERINGHAM

That week he paced familiar floor,
Incapable of much craved sleep,
When late he stalked the silent town
Where all the Godly slept in peace.
The hour had no significance –
He turned to trudge the flint high beach,
Complaining gulls then shouting down
At man's disturbance, out of reach.
He saw the sun hunch up from Earth
Without the slightest breath of heat,
His weary head to vaguely sense
Some consciousness of stumbling feet.
Another wasted day to tread,
Oblivious to people there,
Dread of sleepless nights ahead,
Racked in torment and despair.
His thoughts became entranced at times,
Glimmering back to childhood days,
When freezing seas were warm and calm
In the rippling of tiny waves.
On following nights he'd trawl TV,
Wrapped in duvets for warmth and propped –
Old Westerns, programs on antiques
And glanced half-hearted at the clock.
Or then he'd pass those dark hours on
Around The Common from Curtis Lane,
Taking the path to Coastwatch Point
Without a thought of hail or rain.
Storm had gathered within his life,
The forecast needle moved to "change",
His former course to steer ahead
In youthfulness, had veered in age.
Rising tiredness had breached the shore.
Pressure flooding a surging mind,
The tide had run to lowest ebb
As skies were breaking through to "fine".

Continued

A back-turned sea ignored the man
In planned routines of working days,
The sun was rising warmer then
As nudging through a fading haze.
The beach had reached beyond the flint
To shining sands and bright chalk pools.
The pull of moon on sea and tide
Eclipsed all simple fears of fools.
He chanced upon a coastal bench,
And gazing out toward the sea,
He lay exhausted down to rest,
Still craving that elusive sleep,
When on the seat he read a plaque –
"Horizons make your troubles small" –
And smiling at the truth of that,
His drooping lids began to fall.

# THE COMPULSIVE LITTLE MOVER

My wife has another bee in her bonnet –
So, I just had to write this little sonnet.
Our current house is idyllic to me,
With wonderful views over the sea.
But the kitchen won't take a slow cooker or blender,
So off we go on another bender.
She'd like a cottage, roses round the door,
A spare freezer for the dog food and much, much more,
An enclosed garden for Poppy to roam
And an Aga in the kitchen of our new home.
But I have to say, if left to me –
I'd rather look out over the sea.
But she won't let this matter drop,
So, on behalf of 'self' (as in her) and our dog, Pop,
We appear to be on the move again,
Don't know exactly where or when.
I go with the flow for a peaceful life,
Driven to drink by my lovely wife.
You see, from experiences in the past,
I now know to submit, or be harassed.
Perhaps you think I'm a bit of a wimp
And shouldn't reach out for the demon drink?
But (what a husband!) it's not all about me
Or my incessant love of the sea.
It's just that wish for a peaceful life
And a temporary placation of my dear wife.
'The move' should see off my declining years,
Being out in the sticks, my greatest of fears.
The sound of a tractor to replace the waves,
And car trips to town almost every day.
But please, I beg, don't worry about me
Missing the sound and sight of the sea –
An imminent future of decorating and shopping,
The seaside life I've loved, just stopping.
And in its place 'interior design',
A new quest for cushions and curtains –
                              It's ok, I'm fine!
But secretly, I'm on the brink.
Think I'll have another drink.

Continued

NOTE – ABOUT 18 MONTHS LATER …

Here I sit writing this note in a beautiful cottage with roses round the door, only two miles inland from the sea, in a peaceful country setting. I have to admit, it does seem the best of both worlds, so, through clenched teeth I have to say, "You were right again, darling."

# THE PIT AND THE PENDULUM

Venom-drenched fangs
Curled in their cheeks,
Each coiled to strike
Unleashed as they speak.
Some slithered in
Over the border,
Only "The Charmer"
To call them to "order".
They sit in a place
We should not trust –
That pit is - - - - - - - poisonous!
Outside the big clock ticks
Its straining pendulum swings,
The hammer rises to the bell …
The silence is almost deafening

As the Country waits.

Written at the time of Brexit.

# LEMMINGS

If you were a lemming
Leaping over the cliff,
And half-way down, a voice
Availed you one last wish,
You'd maybe turn back time
Avoiding that abyss,
Wondering why we lemmings
Still behave like this.

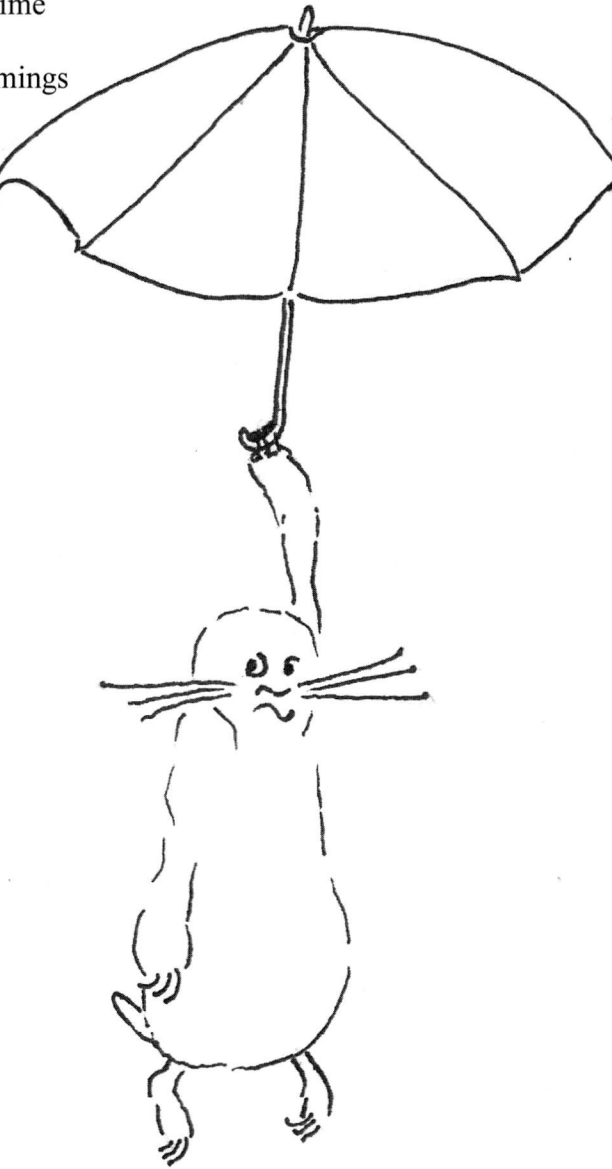

Written during Covid lockdown, following the shameful death of George Floyd.

## 21ST CENTURY MAN

Only the sculptors of hindsight
Can cast the future right,

Reshaping a history of mistakes
From a crucible of greed and hate

To new enlightened times
Moulded in modern designs,

Where statues of past should remain,
As a visible conscience to change,

Until another base is made
From materials awareness gave –

A solid plinth, on which to stand
Twenty-first century man.

# scrapbook

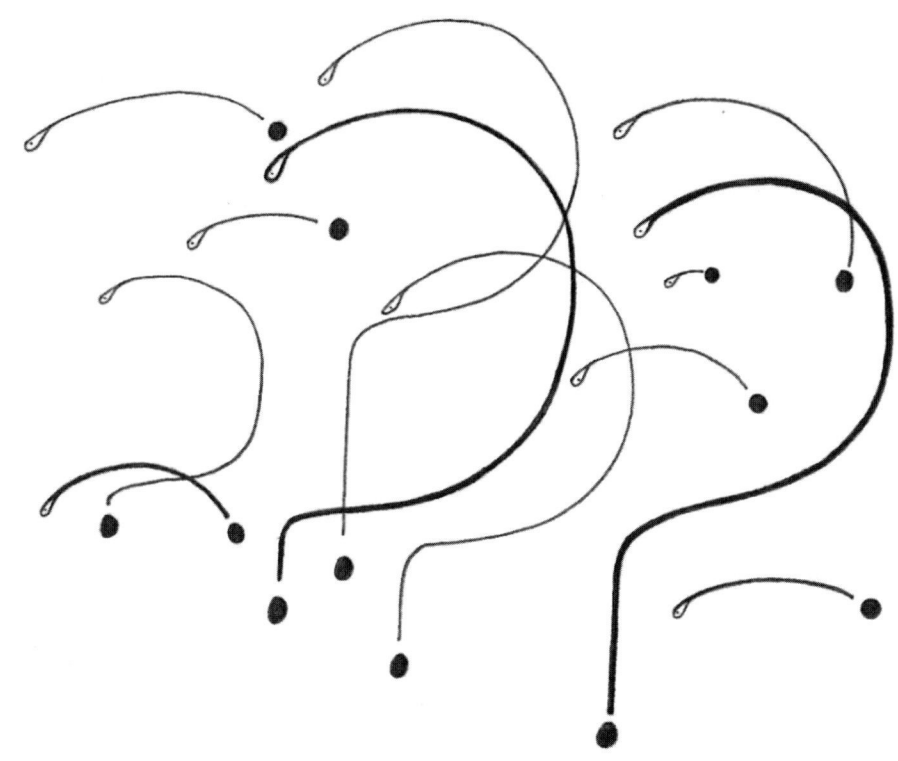

"Bigfoot – o.k., I can live with that but abominable ... NEVER!

# EPILOGUE

If asked why I write poetry, I can honestly say …

I haven't a clue

I just do.

You see – there I go again!

I hope, though, that anyone who has read this book, which is a selection from my published poems, will share some of my journey's memories and, most importantly, will have enjoyed the ride.

SIGNED … The Rhyme Traveller

# INDEX

| PAGE | TITLE |
|------|-------|

SD - #0074 - 120924 - C0 - 254/178/12 - PB - 9781399970594 - Gloss Lamination